The Qing Dynasty

A Captivating Guide to the History of China's Last Empire Called the Great Qing, Including Events Such as the Fall of Beijing, Opium Wars, and Taiping Rebellion

© **Copyright 2019**

All Rights Reserved. No part of this book may be reproduced in any form without permission in writing from the author. Reviewers may quote brief passages in reviews.

Disclaimer: No part of this publication may be reproduced or transmitted in any form or by any means, mechanical or electronic, including photocopying or recording, or by any information storage and retrieval system, or transmitted by email without permission in writing from the publisher.

While all attempts have been made to verify the information provided in this publication, neither the author nor the publisher assumes any responsibility for errors, omissions or contrary interpretations of the subject matter herein.

This book is for entertainment purposes only. The views expressed are those of the author alone, and should not be taken as expert instruction or commands. The reader is responsible for his or her own actions.

Adherence to all applicable laws and regulations, including international, federal, state and local laws governing professional licensing, business practices, advertising and all other aspects of doing business in the US, Canada, UK or any other jurisdiction is the sole responsibility of the purchaser or reader.

Neither the author nor the publisher assumes any responsibility or liability whatsoever on the behalf of the purchaser or reader of these materials. Any perceived slight of any individual or organization is purely unintentional.

Free Bonus from Captivating History (Available for a Limited time)

Hi History Lovers!

Now you have a chance to join our exclusive history list so you can get your first history ebook for free as well as discounts and a potential to get more history books for free! Simply visit the link below to join.

Captivatinghistory.com/ebook

Also, make sure to follow us on Facebook, Twitter and Youtube by searching for Captivating History.

Contents

INTRODUCTION 1
CHAPTER 1 – THE FALL OF THE MING DYNASTY 4
CHAPTER 2 – THE KANGXI EMPEROR 17
CHAPTER 3 – REIGN OF EMPERORS YONGZHENG AND QIANLONG 25
CHAPTER 4 – THE JAHRIYYA REVOLT, WHITE LOTUS REBELLION, AND EIGHT TRIGRAMS UPRISING 33
CHAPTER 5 – THE FIRST OPIUM WAR 39
CHAPTER 6 – THE SECOND OPIUM WAR 48
CHAPTER 7 – TAIPING REBELLION 54
CHAPTER 8 – SELF-STRENGTHENING OF CHINA 65
CHAPTER 9 – EMPRESS DOWAGER CIXI 71
CHAPTER 10 – BOXER REBELLION 80
CHAPTER 11 – THE LAST EMPEROR 88
CONCLUSION 103
REFERENCES 107

Introduction

Qing Dynasty China in 1820

Source: https://en.wikipedia.org/wiki/Qing_dynasty#/media/File:Qing_Dynasty_1820.png

Succeeding the Ming dynasty in 1644, the Qing emperors managed to create one of the largest empires ever to exist in the territories of Asia and the fifth largest empire in the world. The Qing dynasty doubled the size of the Ming territory, but they also more than tripled its population, integrating not just Chinese but also Tibetans, Mongols, Burmese, Tai peoples, and the indigenous people of Taiwan, among others. The Qing dynasty governed this vast empire for nearly 300 years.

The Manchu-centered Qing dynasty was drastically different from other imperial dynasties, as China was observed as only one part of a larger, multinational political entity. The date of the founding of the Qing Empire is much debated as some historians argue it should be 1636, the year of Qing self-proclamation, instead of 1644, which is the year the Qing dynasty conquered Ming China.

The founders of the Qing dynasty were from the Manchu Aisin Gioro clan based in Manchuria, a geographical region that is today shared by China and Russia. The early rulers of the Qing dynasty maintained their Manchu customs, prayed to Buddha, and used the title of "Bogd Khan" instead of Emperor in dealings with the Mongols. They ruled in the Chinese Confucian tradition, proclaiming themselves the "Sons of Heaven" and rulers with the "Mandate of Heaven," meaning they had the blessing of the gods. They also adopted and further developed the existing bureaucracy and administration to help them rule such a vast empire.

The high point of the dynasty was in the late 18th century with the Qianlong Emperor, who boosted China's economy and expanded the empire's territories to its final size. After him, China came under the rule of incompetent leaders who sometimes showed promise but never really returned to the glory of the Qianlong Emperor's empire. The Qing Empire started its steady decline in the late 18th and early 19th centuries. Torn by massive poverty and constant rebellions, China also had to fight foreign forces, mainly Western powers, who sought to colonize China territorially or economically. By this time, the population of the empire rose well above 400 million, but the low tax rate developed a fiscal crisis. Chinese officials became corrupt, and the ruling elite failed to deliver peace. People started questioning the legitimacy of the Qing dynasty and organized uprisings such as the White Lotus Rebellion.

Unable to follow the path to modernization like the rest of the world, China had to face other problems, like the Opium Wars, unprepared. Great Britain led foreign forces against China in order to impose the opium trade, which was prohibited by the Qing emperors. Together with the Taiping Rebellion, these wars cost China around twenty million lives, most of them lost due to famine and poverty. After the wars, China worked hard on restoring itself, as well as modernizing itself with a self-strengthening movement, which was unfortunately disrupted by the First Sino-Japanese War.

Another attempt at modernization, the so-called Hundred Days' Reform, was interrupted by the conservatively-minded Empress Dowager Cixi, an unlikely ruler of Confucian China that regarded women as the possession of men. The Boxer Rebellion followed when foreign religious groups gained the right to convert people and buy property all over China. This violent revolution persuaded Cixi to change her mind and start reforming the empire herself.

After the death of Empress Dowager Cixi, the Qing dynasty rushed to its end. The last emperor was just a boy of six when he had to abdicate. His intriguing life inspired many books, biographies, and even a well-known movie titled *The Last Emperor*. With his death, China lost the image of the great imperial state it once used to be.

Chapter 1 – The Fall of the Ming Dynasty

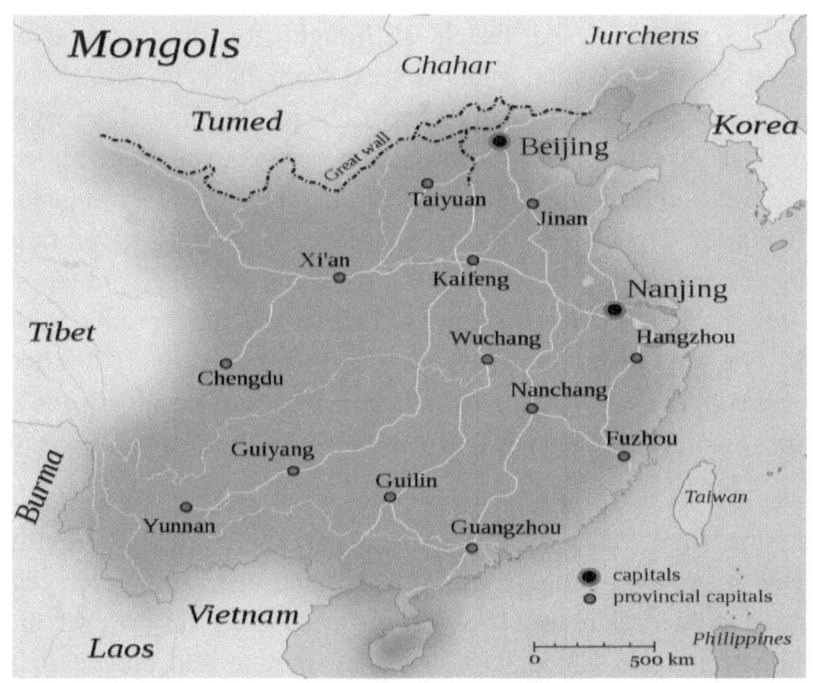

Ming Dynasty China during the 15th century

Source: https://en.wikipedia.org/wiki/Ming_dynasty#/media/File:Ming_Empire_cca_1580_(en).svg

The Ming dynasty ruled China from 1368 until 1644. It originated from the collapse of the Mongol Yuan dynasty and lasted until the famous rebel Li Zicheng took over Beijing in 1644.

During the Ming dynasty, culture flourished. The Yongle Emperor of the Ming dynasty was the one who started the construction of the famous Forbidden City in Beijing, his new capital. It was a complex of royal palaces that would be inhabited by emperors and their court officials until the end of the Qing dynasty and the beginning of the Republic of China. A number of factors influenced the downfall of the Ming dynasty. It mainly started with an economic crisis that involved a sudden lack of silver in the empire. Silver was the main currency with which citizens paid taxes to the emperors.

Portugal, Spain, and the Dutch all fought for monopoly over importing silver in China, which traded them back in silk. Soon, Philip IV, king of Spain and Portugal, began fighting the illegal transport of silver in China. Japan also cut off its supply of silver, which was entering China with the help of Portuguese intermediaries. The Chinese started hoarding the precious silver, thus causing the value of copper to crash. It was impossible to trade in silver anymore, and Chinese farmers had to sell their products for copper but pay taxes in silver they didn't have. In 1630, one thousand copper coins had the value of one ounce of silver. By 1643, the same amount of copper was worth only one-third of an ounce of silver.

During the final years of Ming dynasty rule, in addition to the financial crisis, the climate went through some uncommon changes, making it colder than usual. Some historians call this period the Little Ice Age, and China was struck by famine and plague as a result. The farmers could not produce enough food, and thousands of people died from starvation. Corruption grew in the midst of all this, with state officials bringing even more misery to the suffering people. The city of Huzhou reported a loss of thirty percent of its population due to famine and disease. Other urban centers reported even higher numbers, going as high as fifty percent in the final years of the Ming dynasty. People were leaving villages in search of food. Some roamed the countryside, hoping to find better land for their crops, while others fled to urban areas in hopes of surviving on begging and stealing. Many tried to find sanctuary in large cities as bandit groups started terrorizing the villages. The province of Henan even reported outbreaks of cannibalism in 1640.

Uprisings started all over the country. The common people rebelled because of the new taxes state officials implemented on them. Army leaders that were sent to suppress rebellions often joined them as they were agitated by the lack of food and poor conditions in their ranks. Ethnic minorities, especially Muslims, organized their own rebellions due to oppression and destitution. Some of the uprisings were even religious in nature, like the one that occurred in 1622 when Xu Hongru, a man that authorities believed was an outlawed White Lotus doctrine teacher, gathered the common people and led a rebellion that lasted for over a year.

At the time, Li Zicheng (1606–1645) was one of the most famous bandits in China, and he terrorized the country during the reign of the Chongzhen Emperor (r. 1627–1644). Li operated in the Henan province, where drought caused thousands of people to join him. He accepted two wise advisors in his ranks, which proved to be a valuable addition. Up to that point, Li was known for his cruelty and brutality, but under the influence of his new mentors, he changed his tactics and started treating the people of newly conquered cities fairly. He even exempted them from taxation and showed generosity. These actions are how he earned the title Chuangwang ("Dashing King").

In 1641, Li attacked the Ming dynasty prince Zhu Yousong, Prince of Fu (1607–1646). He took the prince's wealth and gave it to the poor and hungry. By 1643, Li proclaimed himself as Xin Shunwang, the "New Prince of Submission," and started his rule. He organized a new capital city in the Hebei province but soon after spread his rule to the Shaanxi and Shanxi provinces.

In February 1644, Li Zicheng sent a declaration of war to the Chongzhen Emperor of the Ming dynasty, but the message didn't reach the emperor until April of the same year. Historians believe that it was the inadequacy and corruption of the emperor's intelligence service, who failed to convey the message. By the time Li arrived in front of China's capital, Beijing, the royal army was in total disarray. On April 23rd, Li's army walked into the suburbs of Beijing, facing no opposition. He approached the gate of the Forbidden City with a peace offering for the emperor. He stated that he would not only dismiss his rebel forces but that he would also help the Ming dynasty defend itself from any future uprisings. In exchange, Li demanded the emperor recognize him as the official ruler of the Shaanxi and Shanxi provinces, which were already in his possession. For the defense of the dynasty, he demanded a reward of a million ounces of silver. The emperor actually considered this offer but decided to go against it. Li stormed the capital, with the help of two eunuchs named Cao Huashun and Du Xun, who betrayed their emperor. The Chongzhen Emperor committed suicide, and his body was found three days later outside of the northern wall of the Forbidden City.

On April 25th, upon entering the Forbidden City, Li Zicheng declared himself emperor and started the short-lived Shun ("submission") dynasty. Soon after, Li started having trouble controlling his brutal and bloodthirsty generals, among who was Liu Zongmin, a man Li considered to be his "big brother" and best friend. Li faced his generals, commanding them to treat people fairly, but the generals openly defied him. He showed his incompetence as an emperor in pretty much all aspects of ruling the empire, and soon after that incident, the people started resenting him.

Emperor Li decided to deal with the armies of generals who were still loyal to the Ming dynasty, but he encountered severe resistance in the north of the country, which was where the armies of the most powerful general resided. Wu Sangui had around 40,000 regular troops guarding the northern border of the empire. At first, Li tried to gain the general's loyalty, contacting him and offering him a new position in his court. He also tried bribing him, and when that couldn't sway the general, he threatened his family. Wu resisted, and his whole family was slaughtered. Li decided to march directly against the general, but he lost to him twice. The third time, he collected a larger army, counting over 60,000 men and led them himself. Upon hearing that Li Zicheng himself was marching to the Shanhai Pass of the Great Wall, Wu decided to ask the Manchu for help, the very force he was defending China from.

The Manchu was a powerful ethnic group that resided at the northern border of the Ming dynasty territories. They were commonly referred to as the "northern barbarians." Various tribes of different cultural and genealogical heritage were part of the Manchu people, the majority being of Han Chinese origin. They were described by Chinese historians as fierce warriors who valued honor and strength and who do not fear death. The Manchu lived in organized clans, which governed hunting, farming, and warfare. Their religion was shamanistic, and the clan leaders were often regarded as shamans or individuals close to the spirit planes. Only the clan leaders could govern the people in accordance with the will of the spirits.

Earlier in history, the Manchu were known under a different name, Jurchen. They came to power under a man named Nurhaci (1559–1626), a man who united the Jurchen tribes and significantly expanded the domain of his rule. In 1584, Nurhaci began his conquest. Some clans he claimed through marriage alliances, others through military success. He conquered not only other Jurchen clans but also the Mongols and some other minor tribes. His army gathered strength and military proficiency and came to be known by the name the Eight Banners. The main fighting force of the Banners was the company, and it consisted of 300 soldiers. Each soldier was paid a monthly salary, and he also gained a piece of land for his family to work and live on. Companies always consisted of only one ethnicity. United under the Banners, the army was able to preserve its diversity and keep their own cultural identity. The families of soldiers were considered part of the Banners too, and when a woman from one company married a man in another, she simply changed her Banner affiliation.

In 1601, the Eight Banners numbered more than forty companies. In this year, Nurhaci performed a reform of the Banners. Some of the troops he kept for himself, while others he placed under the command of close relatives.

In 1616, Nurhaci took the title of khan and founded the khanate of Later Jin, the same name his ancestors took in 1115. He blamed the Ming dynasty for the deaths of his father and grandfather and started a war with China. By 1621, Nurhaci had conquered eighty Chinese garrisons, the Liaodong province, areas west of Korea, and the territories beyond the Great Wall. With the capture of the city of Liaoyang, Nurhaci assured his control over the lands and paved the path for the future Qing dynasty.

The people of the conquered Chinese territories lived equally with their Jurchen overlords. They were allowed to trade, live, and work freely as any other ethnicity under the united Jurchen clans. But the tension between the Chinese people and the Jurchens was always present. In 1623, the first Chinese uprising took place. Nurhaci easily defeated the rebelling Chinese, but his policy toward them changed. Instead of trying to integrate the Chinese people into the same society, he began separating them into districts and did not allow them to carry weapons. Another small rebellion in 1625/26 was easily quelled, but Nurhaci died that same year.

He was succeeded by his son, Hong Taiji, also written as Huang Taiji (r. 1626–1643). At first, he shared the rule with his three brothers, but in 1629, he showed his military prowess by breaching the Great Wall and occupying the Chinese territories to the west. He took the important cities of Luanzhou, Qian'an, Zunhua, and Yongping. He also worked on disgracing and humiliating his brothers so they would lose their prestige and leave him as the sole ruler. By 1633, he took over all of his brothers' armies and united them under the name of "Three Superior Banners."

Hong Taiji consolidated his power over all the lands his father once ruled, but he abandoned his father's policies. Instead of separating the Chinese population from everyone else, he tried to assimilate them once more. He employed Chinese scholars and advisors, translated Confucius' teachings, and built up a bureaucracy that imitated the one the Ming dynasty had. He did draw on Chinese culture and rituals, but he also founded Jurchen institutions that worked as ministries for Asian relations. The most prominent one was the "Mongol office," which later became a court for diplomatic services within Asian countries.

Ruling over people with different ethnic and cultural backgrounds, Hong Taiji intended to give them a new identity, one that would unite them and put all of the people, no matter their ethnicity, on the same level as the Jurchens. In fact, calling themselves Jurchen became illegal, as the Koreans, Mongols, and Chinese inhabiting his lands were now united under a common name, the Manchu. By having a common name for his people, Hong Taiji hoped to give them national identity and a common goal. In order to promote equality amongst the Manchus, a unique look was welcomed. To distinguish themselves from other Asian peoples, Manchu men shaved the front part of their head while braiding the hair in the back. In addition, Manchu women did not bind their feet like the Chinese women did, as the natural look was more appreciated. The disciplines that were distinctive for the Manchus were horse riding and archery. All peoples that were a part of the Manchus shared common symbols, such as magpies, crows, and a willow tree. They also shared legends and myths. One of the biggest national identity features of the Manchus was shamanism and sacrifices to the heavens, which probably originated from when the Manchu peoples were hunter-gatherers. Shamanism now took a different form, as the Manchus were not nomadic anymore. Instead, they were interested in agriculture and settlements; therefore, shamanism involved large numbers of people taking part in rituals.

The Manchus also had their own language and script. Later, during the reign of the Qing dynasty, the Manchu script was used as the official royal script. State officials and members of the Banners had to be fluent in the Manchu language, but the people commonly used Classical Chinese and Mongolian in everyday life. By 1635, the Manchus produced all of their documents in three languages that were in use throughout most of their state: Manchu, Chinese, and Mongolian. All documents had to be translated in all three languages, but this meant some mistakes were made in translation or through the deliberate censorship of one of the languages. The same documents might have a different form in a certain language, which would leave them open for interpretation.

Now that the Manchus were united under the same cultural and social identity, Hong Taiji started building his empire by establishing the foundation of the rule of the Qing dynasty in 1636.

During 1638, the Banners under the rule of Hong Taiji occupied Korea, making its king renounce his loyalty to the Ming dynasty. With his borders secured, Hong Taiji turned his interests toward China, and he began the long siege of his first target, the strategically important city of Jinzhou. After its fall, Manchu forces turned toward Shanhai Pass. But in September of 1643, Hong Taiji suddenly died. His death stopped the military's progress as a succession dispute started.

In the same year, one of Hong Taiji's young sons named Fulin was crowned as the emperor, but as he was only five years old at the time, it was decided that the regency should be shared by Hong's brother Dorgon and a famous general called Jirgalang.

It was at this time that the Chinese general Wu Sangui was facing the threat of bandit emperor Li Zicheng. The death of the Manchu emperor Hong Taiji gave Wu an opportunity to think over his next move, as he was facing a possible war on two fronts. So, he decided to join forces with the Manchus and face Li's army with their help. Acknowledging the death of the Chongzhen Emperor, Wu wrote to the Manchus, saying that it was the obligation of the Qing dynasty to get rid of the intruder Li Zicheng and dispose of him. In 1644, Wu formally surrendered to the Manchus, agreeing to place his forces in the first combat rows against the army of Li Zicheng.

In the initial confrontation, Wu's forces suffered significant losses, and he would've been defeated if the Manchu army didn't help. Dorgon's Banner outflanked Li's army and broke their ranks. The army of the Shun Empire was forced to retreat beyond the walls of Yongping. They were forced to return to Beijing after their defeat, where they started pillaging the offices and homes of former Ming officials. Li tried one final desperate move to enforce himself as the emperor by conducting a coronation ceremony on May 31st, 1644. However, the day after, he set the Forbidden City ablaze and started retreating to the west, with Wu's troops pursuing him. Soon after, Li Zicheng disappeared and was never again mentioned in history. It is not known what happened to him, but there are several different stories offering an answer, some greatly enhanced by folklore.

In the following months, Dorgon established the rule of the Qing dynasty in Beijing, returning order to the city and promising a reward to anyone who bowed down to the new emperor. Those who would not accept the rule of Manchu would be slaughtered. At first, the people were hesitant to accept a new dynasty, but after being promised prestige and rewards, they soon submitted. The Qing dynasty promised to preserve Chinese cultural heritage but also demanded the people to show submission by adopting the Manchu queue (cue) hairstyle.

A soldier with the Manchu queue hairstyle.

Source: https://en.wikipedia.org/wiki/Queue_(hairstyle)

This act faced resistance among the Han Chinese, who regarded their own hairstyle as a sign of their cultural identity. Mixed with loyalty to the Ming dynasty, this defiance provoked the Manchu to slaughter entire populations in some parts of China. The numbers often went above tens of thousands in just one city, and the stories of these massacres survived for hundreds of years, often serving as fuel for anti-Qing movements, especially during the late 19th and early 20th centuries.

Reforms under the New Qing Dynasty

It took over forty years for the Qing dynasty to consolidate its power over China. Even though they proclaimed equality amongst all the peoples that inhabited the empire, somehow, the Manchus were always the majority when it came to choosing the state and court officials. Dorgon, even though just a regent to the young emperor, became the very embodiment of the state, which gave him more power than any regent ever had. Even the emperor's coronation speech confirmed the power Dorgon wielded. He took several Chinese officials under his own command, showing goodwill to change Manchu supremacy and work more on equality within the empire. Dorgon installed new metropolitan level exams, and every Han Chinese who passed them had a waiting position in the lower

Qing bureaucracy. Thousands of people passed these exams and became civil officials, who served throughout the country.

The military also went through some significant reforms during the rule of Dorgon. He saw the importance of organizing garrisons for the Banners inside China proper (which refers to Inner China without the conquered regions). Between 1644 and 1669, around two million acres of land were distributed to the troops of the Banners and their families. This land consisted of farms, households, and agricultural fields, which families of the men who served the army inhabited and worked. Reports say that 40,000 men and their families serving under the Banners received six acres of land per person inside a single household. Senior officers of the Manchu armies received much larger estates.

Citizens who moved from the original Manchu lands in Liaodong to China organized Manchu enclaves known as Manchu cities. They were described by historians as half-garrison, half-city, where soldiers and their families lived. They served as administrative centers with the looks of ethnical ghettos. These cities weren't standalone cities; they were compounds within the walls of already existing cities, such as Beijing, Xi'an, Nanjing, Hangzhou, and others. In the beginning, only Mongol and Manchu Banners were allowed in metropolitan areas, and they were known as the "capital Eight Banners," while Banners of other ethnicities were known as the "garrison Eight Banners." In 1648, Dorgon ordered that all military Banners within the cities had to physically separate their parts of the city from the Chinese. This is how Beijing had an inner Manchu city surrounding the royal Palace of the Forbidden City, while the Chinese had quarters on the outskirts. The Chinese were allowed to spend time in the inner Manchu part of the city, but they were not allowed to spend the night.

Despite this sharp distinction between Manchu and Chinese districts, the integration of the Chinese people into Manchu culture went well. On the outskirts, the Chinese people were allowed to keep their own traditional cultures alive, but they also chose to implement some

Manchu elements. For example, they performed traditional Chinese theater plays alongside Manchu stories. They inscribed their gates and street signs with Chinese as well as with Manchu scripts, and food served in the outer city was of Chinese and Manchu origin.

With the organization of Manchu garrisons, the Qing dynasty started reorganizing remnants of the old Ming armies, which consisted of Han Chinese. This new fighting force was now serving under the name of the "Green Standard Army." Military historian Luo Ergang estimated that there were around 578,000 Green Standard officers and soldiers in China by 1686. The Green Standard Army was scattered throughout China with the purpose of controlling their countrymen; in other words, Han soldiers controlling other Hans. Initially, the Qing dynasty planned for the Green Standard to maintain local peace and to supervise grain distribution or river transport inside the country. In 1683, a revolt started in China that gave the Green Standard military power within the state, which, thus far, was only reserved for the armies of the Banners.

While the Qing dynasty was setting themselves as rulers in Beijing, the remaining Ming princes tried to maintain the dynasty in exile. Zhu Yousong, Prince Fu, even declared himself emperor, but he was captured and killed within one year of claiming to be one. The last of the Ming princes, Zhu Youlang, tried to avoid death by keeping himself on the move. But in Burma, he was captured by none other than general Wu Sangui and was strangled to death in 1662.

The more serious threat to the Qing dynasty was the Ming loyalist general Zheng Chenggong, better known as Koxinga (1624–1662). He was a naval officer under the Ming dynasty and a fierce anti-Qing advocate. He managed to gather an army counting 250,000 men and around 2,000 ships to oppose the new ruler. His base was around the coastal city Xiamen, also known as Amoy, in the Fujian province. In 1659, Chenggong sailed with his troops into the Yangzi River and defeated the Qing army at Nanjing. However, he chose not to continue with the conquest and stayed at Nanjing, where the Qing sent counterattack forces that defeated Chenggong, who had to retreat back to Xiamen. In order to avoid further conflict with the Qing dynasty, he decided to take the lands of Taiwan and founded what he called "the Ming Eastern Capital." The Qing dynasty responded by prohibiting maritime trade in this area. These draconian measures led to the deaths of many coastal farmers and fishermen. This policy remained in place until 1669, well after the death of Chenggong, because his son and successor, Zheng Jing, managed to keep Taiwan under control and continued to lead anti-Qing forces.

Dorgon died on December 31st, 1650, and a new power struggle for the regency started. The previous co-regent, general Jirgalang, was elected once again, but the Shunzhi Emperor himself, a twelve-year-old boy, started showing his independence and authority, as he had learned about state affairs from his uncle Dorgon. But in order to establish his own supremacy over the Manchu princes and nobles, he had to destroy the reputation of his uncle. Not a week after the funeral procession of Dorgon, the emperor accused him of greed and arrogance.

In order to present himself as a benevolent, wise, Confucian ruler, the emperor started his own reforms within the state. He fought against corruption and extravagance in bureaucratic ranks, and he set up closer supervision of civil officials, both in cities as well as in rural parts. He also invested in agriculture and reduced taxes.

The Shunzhi Emperor ruled the country diligently, and it was due to successful military campaigns that the state was kept together. Those military expeditions were the work of Chinese general Hong Chengchou, who was also the governor of five southern provinces. The emperor indulged himself in culture, theater, calligraphy, and literature, while the power of the courts was actually in the hands of eunuchs and Buddhist priests who surrounded the emperor. The Shunzhi emperor died on February 5th, 1661, at the age of 22, presumably of smallpox.

Chapter 2 – The Kangxi Emperor

Portrait of the Kangxi Emperor, personal name Xuanye

https://en.wikipedia.org/wiki/Kangxi_Emperor

The emperor's death was followed by another power struggle within the court. The deceased emperor's favorite eunuch was accused of forging his will, and he was sentenced to death. However, it was Empress Dowager Xiaozhuang who tempered with the will. The throne was now occupied by the Shunzhi Emperor's third son, who was only seven years old. He had four Manchu seniors acting as his regents, and they held most of the power for the next six years. However, they had to share this power with the emperor's grandmother, now known as Grand Empress Dowager Xiaozhuang. The new emperor's personal name was Xuanye, and it was decided he should inherit the throne because he survived an outbreak of smallpox when he was much younger. As emperor, he was known by the name Kangxi ("peaceful, congenial"). In Chinese history, he is known as the longest-ruling emperor, occupying the throne for 61 years. He is also considered to be one of the greatest emperors China ever had.

Almost immediately after he became emperor, his regents, led by military commander Oboi, started a series of changes in the existing government. They replaced the beloved eunuchs of the Shunzhi Emperor with Manchu officials in the top bureaucratic positions. They also made an official institution out of the already existing Imperial Household Department, which would be the most significant tool for implementing imperial policies after 1661. The regents also expanded the power of the Court of Colonial Affairs and the Deliberative Council of Princes, which now had control over both military and civil affairs, while diminishing the power of the Censorate and the Hanlin Academy. The Censorate was a supervisory agency of China that employed bureaucrats who were tasked with monitoring the behavior of all court visitors, officials, and even the emperor. Their job was to make sure all protocols were followed but also prevent any possible corruption from occurring. The Hanlin Academy employed only elite scholars who performed all secretarial and literary tasks for the emperor. Artists who worked for the court were also a part of this academy.

The regents' only goal was to preserve the Manchus at the top of the social order; in other words, they wanted to ensure they remained superior to any other ethnicity within the empire. In order to achieve this, they managed to stop the emperor from learning Chinese. Instead, they focused the Kangxi Emperor's studies on Manchu military arts and Manchu scripts. Later, during his adult life, the emperor did learn Chinese with the help of eunuchs.

Later, the Kangxi Emperor was resentful of his regents and tried to undermine them and bring their power down, with the help of both Chinese and Manchu supporters. The emperor tried to reverse some of the changes in government that the regents implemented, but it was only in 1669 that he moved directly against them. Oboi was accused of arrogance and dishonesty and was arrested. He soon after died in prison, and his supporters were punished, some with a death sentence, others with much milder punishments. From this point onward, the Kangxi Emperor took firm control over his lands and finally became the sole ruler.

Revolt of the Three Feudatories

During the early years of the Kangxi Emperor's rule, he had to deal with a rebellion known as the Revolt of the Three Feudatories, also known as the Rebellion of Wu Sangui.

During the Manchu conquest of China, Wu Sangui earned the respect of the future Qing emperors. He was given the title "Pingxi Prince" (West Pacifying Prince), as well as the Yunnan and Guizhou provinces to govern. But he wasn't the only ex-Ming general who deserved titles and lands for helping the Manchus set up the Qing dynasty. Shang Kexi and Geng Zhongming both received similar titles, as well as the provinces of Guangdong and Fujian to rule. These three princes enjoyed far more freedom than any other governor. They were allowed to choose their own state officials, to have their own armies, and to set up their own tax systems.

These three feudatories put a constant strain on imperial resources. They alone emptied half of the royal treasury. Shang Kexi and Geng Zhongming and their successors ruled as tyrants, oppressing their people and giving too much freedom to their generals to collect food and money from commoners. Because of this, the Kangxi Emperor felt threatened and wanted to regulate their power.

In 1673, Shang Kexi asked the emperor for permission to retire. Soon after, Wu Sangui and Geng Jingzhong, the grandson of Geng Zhongming, did the same. Court officials advised the emperor not to grant them their wishes, but the Kangxi Emperor took the advice of his grandmother and granted retirement to all three generals, ordering them to resettle in Manchuria. They refused to obey this order, and instead, they chose to rebel against the Qing dynasty. That same year, Wu Sangui denounced the Qing dynasty and proclaimed himself the founder of the new Zhou dynasty. He convinced the Chinese people to join him, promising the return of the values of the Ming dynasty. He cut off his Manchu queue and restored some of the old Ming customs, which helped him gain the trust of some of the Han Chinese officials. Wu sent messages to the Kangxi Emperor, saying he would let him live and not bother him if he would leave Beijing and return to his old Manchu lands. The emperor refused this proposal and thus ignited an eight-year-long war against the rebel forces.

In 1674, Wu took control of the Hunan and Sichuan provinces. The provinces of Fujian, Guangdong, Guangxi, and Shaanxi also joined the revolt. The Kingdom of Tungning in Taiwan also joined, and their ruler, Zheng Jing, allegedly brought 150,000 men to the shores of the Guangdong province.

Wu died in August 1678 and was succeeded by his grandson, Wu Shifan, who ordered the rebel army to retreat to Yunnan. Wu Sangui's death diminished the morale of the rebel forces, and the Kangxi Emperor took the opportunity to retake control over the province of Hunan. In 1680, the Han Chinese Green Standard Army took over Sichuan and southern Shaanxi territories, with Manchu forces providing logistics and provisions. Soon, the Qing dynasty reclaimed the territories of Guizhou and Guangxi, forcing Wu Shifan to retreat to Kunming.

In 1681, the general of the imperial forces, Zhao Liangdong, led a three-pronged attack on Yunnan with the armies of Hunan, Guangxi, and Sichuan. They conquered Mount Wuhua and besieged Kunming.

In October, the city fell, and Wu Shifan committed suicide. His rebel army surrendered immediately after his death. But the final victory over the rebels was the Qing's conquest of the Kingdom of Tungning in Taiwan in 1683, which was when Taiwan finally came under the rule of the Qing Empire. The last ruler of the Kingdom of Tungning, Zheng Keshuang, was given the title Duke Haicheng, and his army was incorporated into the Eight Banners.

The Post-Revolution Period

After the Revolt of the Three Feudatories, the Kangxi Emperor turned his attention to the northern borders of his lands, where constant clashes between Russians (Cossacks) and Manchu Mongols occurred. By 1683, all the Russian garrisons in the area were destroyed, except for Albazin. The emperor's plan was to gather such a large army that it would intimidate the Russians and make them less willing to fight. In 1685, he began the siege of Albazin. It wasn't long before this fortified village surrendered. The Qing emperor had ordered the wooden walls of the settlement to be set ablaze, and as soon as they started piling up dry wood, the Russians surrendered. Around 600 Russian defenders were allowed to retreat to Nerchinsk, but some chose to join the Qing army and settle in a Russian enclave in Beijing. The Qing forces burned the settlement of Albazin, but they did not destroy the crops around it before leaving. Hearing about the defeat, Moscow sent emissaries to China to negotiate peace, but it would take some time for these emissaries to arrive.

Hearing that the Qing forces abandoned Albazin and that there were crops to be harvested there, the Russians returned. They reinforced the walls with earth and settled once again, hoping that the Chinese were gone forever. But the Qing army returned and began another siege of the village in July 1686. The Russians resisted, as they had gathered the harvest and had enough food to last them until spring, but they did not have enough water. The siege lasted until early winter when, finally, news of the traveling Moscow emissaries' arrival in Beijing reached them. The emperor ordered the siege of

Albazin to temporarily halt while waiting for the negotiations to begin. But at that time, only around 66 out of the original 826 Russian soldiers remained in the fortress, the rest having died due to disease caused by the lack of fresh water. By December, there were only around twenty men left in Albazin. The Kangxi Emperor only ordered the retreat of his forces in 1687 when he heard that the Russian ambassador had arrived in Mongolia.

In 1689, a treaty was signed. This was the first treaty between the Qing dynasty and Russia. It is called the Treaty of Nerchinsk, and according to the terms, the Russians had to give up all the territories north of the Amur River, but they got to keep the areas between the Argun River and Lake Baikal.

The outer Mongolians were independent of Manchu rule, but they did pay tribute to the Qing emperor. A conflict between the Khalkha Mongols and the Dzungar Khanate (which was ruled by the Oirat Mongols) arose. Galdan Boshugtu Khan attacked Khalkha, invading the territory from the west. So, Khalkha's royal family crossed the Gobi Desert and sought help from the Qing dynasty. The Kangxi Emperor answered, and in 1690, the Qing forces met the forces of the Dzungar Khanate in the Battle of Ulan Butung in Inner Mongolia. The Qing forces were victorious, but this wasn't the end of the troubles in Mongolia. In 1696, the Kangxi Emperor personally led the Qing armies in another campaign against the Dzungar Khanate, in what is known as the Dzungar-Qing Wars that took decades to end (1687–1757). The victory of the Qing in these conflicts led to the incorporation of Mongolia, Tibet, Qinghai, and Xinjiang regions into the Qing Empire. The conflict also resulted in the eradication of most of the Dzungar Khanate's population.

During all this warfare, the Kangxi Emperor worked on bringing more Han Chinese into the politics of the state. He organized a special examination for the "Great Confucians of Broad Learning" in 1679, and he invited 188 Han Chinese scholars to participate. More than thirty refused the invitation, but fifty of those who attended passed the exams, and all of them received positions as state officials.

The Kangxi Emperor was a tolerant, patient, cautious, and pragmatic ruler who did not favor either Manchu or Chinese officials. He tried to promote equality and set an atmosphere of inclusiveness throughout his empire. He also gave special attention to develop efficient administrative institutions on a local level. In crisis situations, the Kangxi Emperor relied on "special commissioners" elected for their competence. He was surrounded by loyal eunuchs, bodyguards, and both Manchu and Chinese supporters. He set up an institution called the "Palace Memorial," which allowed his state officials, both within the capital and in the provinces, to communicate with him directly, using special messengers.

He also paid special attention to touring his empire, a tradition that was ignored during the early ages of the Qing dynasty rule. By devoting time to visit parts of his empire, the emperor could see for himself how it was being governed, as well as allowing to be seen by the general population, thus creating a stronger relationship between himself and his officials. In the period between 1681 and 1722, a total of 128 such tours of the Kangxi Emperor were recorded. These tours were often depicted by artists and described in literature. They were an amazing opportunity to promote both Manchu and Chinese cultures and bring them closer to each other.

After 1683, the rule of the Kangxi Emperor was relatively peaceful and productive. Another way to sway the Han Chinese who were loyal to the Ming was to slowly introduce them amongst Qing officials by allowing their scholars to work without being officially part of the imperial bureaucratic system. He also ordered a dictionary of Chinese symbols to be made and employed the Han Chinese to work on it. Involving them in the cultural achievements of the empire pushed them to gradually accept the Qing rule.

The Kangxi Emperor showed great interest in Western technology and culture, which entered China through the Jesuits. He employed

Jesuits as teachers, medics, and scholars, and they worked on astronomy projects, the mapping of the Great Chinese Empire, and as artists at the Qing court. One of the prominent Jesuits of the Kangxi Emperor's court was Karel Slavicek, a Czech missionary who was employed to create the first detailed map of Beijing. He also taught the emperor how to play the spinet. The Kangxi Emperor was the first Chinese emperor who actually played a Western instrument. Slavicek worked in the fields of astronomy and mathematics in China, but he also wrote a treatise on Chinese music. Unfortunately, this document did not survive.

The Kangxi Emperor died on December 20th, 1722. After his death, another power struggle started, this one known under the name of the Nine Lords' War. During his life, the Kangxi Emperor groomed his second surviving son, Yinreng, for succession, naming him as the crown prince. But the boy had a cruel nature. Yinreng would often beat and kill his servants and was known to engage in pedophilic acts. He also indulged in a sexual relationship with his father's concubines, which, at that time, was considered incest. Seeing his son's nature, the Kangxi Emperor had no other choice but to revoke his titles and place him under house arrest in 1707. Later, blaming mental illness for his son's actions, he restored his titles in 1709. Yinreng's supporters tried to take over the throne while the emperor was on his last tour to the south of the country in 1712. The emperor had left state affairs to his son, but hearing of a possible coup, he rushed back to Beijing, where he placed his son under house arrest yet again. The emperor then vowed he would not name any of his sons as crown prince. Instead, he would place the name of his successor in his will, which would be opened only after his death.

While on his deathbed, the Kangxi Emperor gathered some of his sons around him, and it was declared that it was the fourth prince, Yinzhen, who would succeed him. Yinzhen was soon crowned, and he began his rule as the Yongzheng Emperor.

Chapter 3 – Reign of Emperors Yongzheng and Qianlong

Portrait of the Yongzheng Emperor (left) and the Qianlong Emperor (right)

Source: https://en.wikipedia.org/wiki/Yongzheng_Emperor

There is much controversy around the succession of the Yongzheng Emperor. Some of his brothers accused him of forging his father's will and inheriting the throne illegally. During his rule, the Yongzheng Emperor was constantly paranoid of his brother's intentions. Yinzhi, the third eldest brother, had been under house arrest for supporting ex-crown prince Yinreng, who had died two years after his father.

In order to prevent any plots against him, the Yongzheng Emperor separated his eighth brother, Yinsi, from his supporters. He gave Yinsi the highest possible titles, making him the equivalent of today's prime ministers. Yinsi became Prince Lian of the First Rank, minister of the Feudatory Affairs Office, and the top-ranking member of the royal council. In order to keep Yinsi away from his political associates and make it impossible for them to conspire, the emperor sent them away on different tasks around the country. Some were sent on military campaigns, some were stripped of their titles, and some were sent away to live in exile. However, in 1724, the emperor publicly stripped Yinsi of all his titles, accusing him of purposely mishandling an assignment. Yinsi was then placed under house arrest and forced to take a degrading name "Acina" or "Akina," which can be translated as either a pig or a frozen fish, although some historians argue it is a Chinese transcription of the Manchu word "Aqina," which can be translated as "to carry (a crime)."

The rule of the Yongzheng Emperor was despotic but efficient. It was peaceful and prosperous. It is said that the Yongzheng Emperor wanted to create an efficient empire with minimal expenses, and he was ruthless when it came to eradicating corruption. In order to allow provinces to bloom, he implemented tax exemptions, which lasted five to ten years and allowed local populations to prosper. But these tax exemptions were conditioned. Local governments had to compete in buying agricultural lands. Whichever province bought the most would win the tax exemption. Sometimes, the local officials would lie about the acquired farming lands in hopes of winning, and this is where the emperor's despotic rule and anti-corruption efforts were the most visible.

Furthermore, in order to be more inclusive of ethnic minorities, the Yongzheng Emperor allowed all ethnicities living in China to take civil service exams. This act was even spread from urban environments to rural provinces. The emperor also built orphanages for the increasing number of parentless children. The orphanages weren't funded by local governments or even by the royal dynasty itself. They worked on a system of donations made by wealthy people. They served less as help for poor citizens and more as a model of how the wealthy should act toward the impoverished.

The Yongzheng Emperor ruled for only 13 years before he died at the age of 56. He died suddenly while reading official state documents. Because his death was so sudden, it inspired various legends, the most notable one being that he was killed by Lu Siniang, the daughter or granddaughter of the prominent Chinese poet Lu Liuliang, who wrote against the Qing dynasty and was punished for it. In reality, the cause of the emperor's death was a lethal amount of an elixir of immortality, which he consumed in order to prolong his life. Chinese elixirs of immortality often contained large doses of mercury and arsenic; therefore, drinking this elixir was a constant threat to one's life.

In order to prevent a succession dispute, like the one he had to face when he inherited the throne, the Yongzheng Emperor ordered his third son to commit suicide because this son supported Yinsi, his uncle. The emperor wrote down the name of his successor on two separate papers and hid them in two separate places. Upon his death, when they unsealed the documents and if the names matched on both papers, the officials would know that there were no forging attempts or trickery during the reading of his will. Both papers read the name of his fourth son, Hongli.

The ascension of Hongli to the throne came as no surprise. He was the emperor's favorite son and was the favorite grandson of the previous emperor, Kangxi. Upon ascension to the throne, Hongli took the name Qianlong, which means "Lasting Eminence." He ruled from 1735 until 1796 when he abdicated in an attempt not to rule longer than his grandfather, the Kangxi Emperor. But he kept the power over the empire as a retired emperor until he died in 1799.

The Qianlong Emperor was a great military leader, and he had to put his skills to use as soon as he took the crown. In 1735, the Miao Rebellion in southwest China broke out, as the people were unsatisfied by the local administration and extortion. The Qianlong Emperor sent a bloodthirsty general named Zhang Guangsi to quell the rebellion. The Qing forces killed approximately 18,000 rebels and destroyed around 1,200 Miao fortifications.

During the reign of the Qianlong Emperor, the Dzungar Khanate finally fell under Chinese rule and was renamed Xinjiang. Mongol Buddhists of the Dzungar Khanate rebelled against Qing rule in 1755. However, the Qing forces crushed the rebellion in 1758, destroying the last great nomadic empire in Asia. The victory over the Dzungar Khanate wasn't enough for the Qianlong Emperor, as he ordered their mass extermination. Therefore, the Dzungar people ceased to exist as a people, although it is said that around twenty percent of them fled to Russia, where they were assimilated into the Kazakh tribes.

The Qianlong Emperor wasn't as successful in the war with Burma, known as the Sino-Burmese War (1765–1769). He thought the victory would be easy, and he only sent the Green Standard Army from the Yunnan province, which was on the border of Burma. The Qing army did not have enough people to fight the battle-hardened Burmese warriors. There were several attempts to penetrate deeper into Burmese territory by the Qing forces, but only the third invasion came close to victory. In the end, they, too, failed due to unfamiliar terrain and tropical diseases that wiped out their army. In 1769, the situation was bad enough for both sides, and they finally reached an agreement. However, China kept provoking Burma by keeping heavy military forces on its borders and preventing trade for nearly two decades. War did not happen, though, because Burma asked for a diplomatic solution to the ongoing problem in 1790. China regarded this act as a Burmese surrender and proclaimed victory.

The situation in Vietnam was also unsuccessful. The last leader of the Le dynasty, Le Chieu Thong, faced a rebellion led by his three brothers. He ran to China, where he asked the Qianlong Emperor for protection and help to gain his throne back. The Qing emperor agreed and sent his army to Tang Long, the capital of Vietnam. The city was conquered in 1788, but Qing forces were surprised by the rebel attack on New Year's Eve, who crushed the Chinese army and retook the capital. The Qianlong Emperor kept Le Chieu Thong and his whole family under his protection, but the Qing dynasty did not meddle in Vietnamese affairs for the next ninety years.

Even though the Chinese forces were less successful in the south, the Qianlong Emperor nearly doubled the territories his forefathers held. He conquered many non-Han Chinese peoples, such as the Uyghurs, Kazakhs, the Kyrgyz people, Mongols, and others. He brought them all under one single rule, that of the great Qing dynasty. All of these military expeditions took its toll on the royal treasury, as it was expensive maintaining such a large army. In time, this took a toll on military numbers as well, as the Qing army started to decline.

In 1765, the Ush rebellion started. The Manchu official Sucheng and his son had repeatedly raped Muslim Uygur women. For a long time, the Uygur people harbored their anger toward the Qing officials. Finally, they rebelled and gathered enough men to attack. The Qianlong Emperor ordered the destruction of Uyghur settlements, and the royal army enslaved their women and children and slaughtered all the men.

During peaceful times, when all the wars were over, the generals did not see any reason to continue training the army. Instead, they indulged in a lavish lifestyle. The military officials caused the Qing army to degrade even more. This might be the reason why the Qianlong Emperor would later be unable to quell the White Lotus

Rebellion, which started at the end of his rule and continued through the rule of his successor, the Jiaqing Emperor.

The Establishment of the Grand Council

At the beginning of the Qing dynasty, political power was in the hands of eight princes and a number of Manchu officials, who also served as royal councilors. Established in 1637, this council was handling most of the major issues in the Qing Empire. At some point, the power of this council was such that they could even overrule the emperor and even depose him. In 1643, the Shunzhi Emperor included Han Chinese in the council. But with the establishment of the Southern Study and the Grand Council, the power of the council of princes diminished, and it completely stopped existing in 1717.

The Southern Study was established by the Kangxi Emperor in 1677. Its name, the Southern Study, was due to its location, which was in the southwestern part of the Palace of Heavenly Purity, where the emperor's audience hall was. This location was chosen because the emperor would have easy access to his councilors whenever he needed them. The Southern Study held the most political power until the Grand Council was established. It still remained an important institution until it was abolished in 1898, but it never again had the role of council. Even in modern Chinese, the term "access to the Southern Study" means that someone has great influence, but it also means he came to be influential through unofficial paths.

The Qing Grand Council was founded in 1738 by the Qianlong Emperor, who dismantled the existing Interim Council, which had been founded by his father to help him rule. The Grand Council controlled many segments of the Qing dynasty's rule. Not only did they advise the emperor in times of need, but they were also in charge of drafting all edicts, taking care of the emperor's transportation, and planning and overseeing various ceremonies and celebrations that would involve the emperor and his family. They also took many administrative responsibilities, but they maintained a degree of freedom and were not restrained by the same laws that applied to the outer circle of the palace or even the provinces.

The Jiaqing Emperor, the son of the Qianlong Emperor, was the one who made the first changes within the Grand Council. He limited the number of councilors and introduced punishments for those who made administrative errors. In 1861, during the regency of Empress Dowagers Ci'an and Cixi, the Grand Council held the most power. Since both empress dowagers had no experience in state affairs, the Grand Council made the majority of the decisions. They even issued an edict that officially granted them such power. The Grand Council lasted until 1911 when the Prince-Regent at the time, Prince Chun, abolished it in favor of an "Imperial Cabinet."

Cultural Achievements

The Qianlong Emperor was proud of his Manchu heritage and worked vigorously to preserve it. The Qianlong Emperor saw the Manchu culture as a moral code that led the Qing dynasty to power. He even issued an order for a book of Shamanic code collections, which would later be published in *Siku Quanshu*, the largest collection of Chinese books that numbers 10,680 titles. The *Siku Quanshu* was also the largest project of the Qianlong Emperor. He gathered an elite team of China's best scholars and tasked them with collecting, editing, and printing the incredibly large collection on Chinese philosophy, culture, history, and literature. The project didn't only want to show off the Manchu culture. It was also a way of controlling political opponents, as all the books in private libraries were carefully examined. The books that did not suit the current political structure of the state were scheduled for destruction, but not until they were carefully indexed.

Around 2,300 books were issued for total destruction and another 360 for censorship or partial destruction. The goal was to suppress any anti-Qing teachings that could cause a rebellion or be used as propaganda against the royal dynasty. Completing the *Siku Quanshu* took approximately ten years, during which over 150,000 books were destroyed or banned. Many went through the harsh process of censorship, where parts of the texts were completely removed. The worst destiny was reserved for the books published during the Ming dynasty, which were all burned.

The authors of certain books were also prosecuted. If the inquisition found as little as one sentence that could be interpreted as cynical toward the rule of the Qing dynasty, the author would be punished. There are 53 known cases of literary prosecution done by the inquisition. The authors were punished in various ways, the most common being decapitation or slow slicing, which was a slow process of inflicting many cuts that would bleed and eventually kill the prisoner, or in case they were already dead, body mutilation.

The Qianlong Emperor was a great writer himself. He was very productive when it came to poetry and essays. Between 1749 and 1800, he wrote over 40,000 poems and 1,300 essays, which makes him an incredibly productive author, even by modern standards. His poems were mostly odes, glorifying a place or a person. It is a Chinese literary tradition to praise a particular object, and the Qianlong Emperor used this tradition to link his name to certain places and events.

Besides creating art in the form of literature, the Qianlong Emperor was passionate about collecting it as well. The Qing dynasty, like any other, served as a patron of the arts, and all the emperors were proud of their royal collections. However, the Qianlong Emperor took the practice to another level, as he confiscated private collections of other nobles by any means possible. He also vigorously followed the art market and employed special advisors who would point out significant artworks worthy of collection. This royal collection became a part of the emperor's private life. On his many travels, he would bring paintings of landscapes just to be able to compare them with the actual landscapes of the places he visited. He often added a verse or a whole poem to a certain painting, and he also kept private notes about the artworks he especially enjoyed, almost like a private diary.

Chapter 4 – The Jahriyya Revolt, White Lotus Rebellion, and Eight Trigrams Uprising

In 1781, street violence became common between two branches of an Islamic mysticism group, the Jahriyya Sufi Muslims and the Khafiyya Sufi Muslims. The fighting happened in northwest China, more specifically, in the Qinghai and Gansu provinces. To prevent further unrest and constant lawsuits between the Khafiyya and Jahriyya Sufi Muslims, Qing officials arrested Ma Mingxin, the founder of the Chinese Jahriyya order.

Agitated by the arrest of their leader, the Jahriyyans revolted. The Qing forces were joined by Khafiyya Sufis and the Gedimu school of Islam, while the Jahriyyans had the support of a number of Han Chinese.

Ma Mingxin was kept in Lanzhou, the capital of the Gansu province, and the Jahriyyans decided to besiege the city in order to rescue their leader. In hopes of appeasing the rebellious people, the Chinese officials decided to show them that Ma Mingxin was alive by bringing him to the city walls. Upon seeing their chained leader, the Jahriyyans showed nothing by devotion to their leader and tried to rescue him with even more effort. Scared by the acts of the rebels, the Qing officials immediately executed Ma Mingxin.

In order to suppress further rebellions, the Qing emperor decided to exile the Jahriyya people to the territory of Xinjiang, more specifically, in the northern regions of Dzungaria. They were not allowed to resettle anywhere else, not even into other regions of Xinjiang. Ma Mingxin's widow and his children were also exiled to Dzungaria after his death.

Another rebellion took place from 1796 until 1804; this one was initiated by the White Lotus movement, a secret religious organization. The reason for the uprising was the amount of taxes they had to pay. The rebellion started in the mountainous regions nestled between the Sichuan, Hubei, and Shaanxi provinces.

The White Lotus was a religious movement that was especially appealing to the Han Chinese, as it worshiped Wusheng Laomu (the "Unborn Venerable Mother"), a deity that promised to gather all her children into one family at the turn of the century. The White Lotus had roots in both Buddhism and Manichaeism, the latter being a religious movement in the Sasanian Empire. The doctrine of the White Lotus prohibited any meat-oriented diet, as vegetarianism was favored. It also allowed men and women of the faith to engage freely in relationships of any kind, which was a shocking act for traditional China. The White Lotus was considered a heterodox religious sect during the Mongol rule of China, which banned the movement and drove its members underground.

The White Lotus became a symbol of national and religious resistance all over the empire. They were initiators and participators of various small rebellions since their forming in the early 13th century. The Qing dynasty confirmed their ban and published an edict that placed any secret religious society that was not approved by the state in the same position as the White Lotus. All gatherings with the intention of celebrating non-official religious movements were illegal and therefore prosecuted under the full extent of the law.

The White Lotus Rebellion in 1796 had a forerunner, a small rebellion that broke out in 1774 under the leadership of Wang Lun, an expert in martial arts and herbal healing. He had several thousands of followers who he managed to persuade in thinking that he was the reincarnation of Maitreya, a future Buddha sent to prepare the path for the new emperor, and that it was his destiny to become the emperor of China. He led the attack on the city of Shouzhang in the western Shandong province on October 3rd, 1774. After ransacking the treasury and granary, they abandoned it and moved to attack another city, Yangku, where the local garrison had recently left to help free the previously conquered Shouzhang. After capturing Yangku, the rebel forces moved to attack the strategically important city of Linqing. On their way there, they had several encounters with the army of the Qing dynasty, but the rebels were victorious each time. Wang Lun's forces besieged the city of Linqing for several days before ultimately being surrounded and crushed by the Qing army. It is said that Wang Lun did not want to be captured alive and that he committed suicide by setting himself on fire. His body was recognized only by his sword and bracelets. Wang Lun probably failed in this attempt because he could not gain the trust of his followers. Seeing himself as the next emperor, he did not promise lower taxes, and he did not distribute captured wealth or food. He kept everything for himself and demanded blind obedience from his followers. Often, he would force civilians to join his army by threatening their families.

The later White Lotus Rebellion in 1796 was of a much larger scale. The White Lotus was joined by the impoverished people of the region in their uprising against the high taxes. The rebellion quickly grew in numbers, but it also spread to the surrounding regions and became a serious threat to the Qing government.

The Qianlong Emperor sent two generals, Helin and Fuk'anggan, to suppress the rebellion, but both of them were inefficient to the point that the unorganized rebel forces managed to defeat them. They both died in battle in 1796. The fighting continued, and it was only in

1800 that the Chinese Qing officials implemented new tactics. Local militias were organized to help the Qing army surround and defeat the White Lotus rebels. During the rule of the Qianlong Emperor, a law was passed that stated the Eight Banner armies were never to fight internal battles and rebellions; therefore, the Chinese government had to rely only on the Han Chinese Green Standard Army.

The White Lotus forces used guerrilla tactics, and the Qing generals often complained that they could not identify the rebels in the midst of the local population. Because the rebels wore no distinctive markings, the whole population suffered at the hands of the Qing army. Because of the brutality the Qing forces showed toward the people, they gained a new nickname, the "Red Lotus Society."

The rebellion was finally quelled in 1805 when the Qing emperor sent 7,000 men of the Banner army, who helped the Green Standard Army and the local militia to pursue and eradicate the rebel forces. A pardon was offered to any deserter of the White Lotus in hopes it would weaken their ranks. The Qing administrators continued to pursue the members of the White Lotus even after the rebellion was successfully suppressed. They also destroyed any manuscripts or other items that were linked to the ideology of the White Lotus.

In 1812, the leaders of the Eight Trigram Sect, which was a branch of the White Lotus, declared 1813 as the year for a rebellion. They wanted to overthrow the Qing dynasty, claiming that Li Wencheng, one of their leaders, was the true Ming successor. Another leader of the same sect, Lin Qing, declared himself to be the reincarnation of Maitreya. Followers of the Eight Trigram Sect believed he would be the one who would remove the Qing emperor, who, in their beliefs, had lost the Mandate of Heaven. The third leader of the rebellion was Feng Keshan, a legendary martial artist who had little to no interest in religion. The three leaders met in 1811 when the appearance of a comet occurred. They took it as a sign of the end of the Qing dynasty, although Beijing regarded it as a sign of the Qing dynasty's long rule and prosperity.

In 1812, the leaders of the movement started recruiting their followers to build an army and gathered donations from ordinary people. They promised ranks and other rewards after the success of the rebellion to the people who donated money or food to their cause. However, the sharp increase in the price of wheat, which was often prompted by floods and droughts, was what truly inspired people to join the rebellion. The leaders chose September 15th for the beginning of their rebellion, as the harvest would have just ended, which would instigate even more people to join their ranks. The other reason was that the Jiaqing Emperor would be out of Beijing on a hunt, leaving Beijing with minimal guards. The plan was to take Beijing and assassinate the emperor when he would return to his palace.

However, rumors of the rebellion reached Beijing, and Li Wencheng was arrested on September 2nd, 1813. He was tortured during his imprisonment, but before he was executed, he was saved by his followers, who broke into the prison. This event sped up the planned rebellion, which actually started on September 6th. The rebel forces were quick to take the towns of Huaxian, Caoxian, and Dingtao in the Zhili and Shandong provinces.

The attack on the Forbidden City was a mixed success. Although around eighty rebels managed to enter through the gates before they were closed, it wasn't enough to win the fight. Lin Qing was in charge of the assault on Beijing, but he did not fight in the actual battle. His plan was to hide rebels in shops around the walls of the Forbidden City and wait for noon when the gate guards would go for a meal. The rebels wore white headbands and waist belts to distinguish themselves from common citizens. Prince Mianning, who would later become the Daoguang Emperor in 1820, joined the fight inside the walls of the Forbidden City, and his presence boosted the morale of the Qing forces, which successfully crushed the rebellion.

The rebels fled the battlefield and were pursued by the princes themselves, as well as by some eunuchs from the royal palace and officers of the Imperial Guards Brigade. For several more months, the rebels were successful in keeping some of the towns under siege, but finally, the Qing forces crushed the rebellion entirely on January 14th, 1814.

Li Wencheng retreated to the city of Huixian with approximately 4,000 of his followers. There, he committed suicide when the city was besieged by the Qing forces. His wife, Li Zhangshi, continued to resist the siege and kept the city closed until the following year. As the city walls were breached by the Qing army, she hanged herself.

Chapter 5 – The First Opium War

Battle between the Chinese and the British forces during the First Opium War

https://en.wikipedia.org/wiki/First_Opium_War

By 1820, China had the largest economy in the world. But by the end of the Opium Wars, its gross domestic product (GDP) fell by half, making it difficult for the government to recover from this economic disaster until well after World War II. The Opium Wars were fought in the mid-19th century between China and the British

Empire, which had imposed the trade of opium on China. Various treaties were proposed by the British government to China that were only meant to weaken the power of the ruling Qing dynasty, which also had the consequence of weakening China's sovereignty over its territories.

Opium was known and used in China as early as the 7th century but only as a medicinal remedy. For recreational use, it was rarely used due to its high price. Opium was introduced to Asia by Arab merchants. The first significant ban on opium happened during the Qing dynasty in 1729 when the product named madak was labeled illegal. Madak was powdered opium mixed with tobacco and was intended for smoking. The main shipments of opium came into China from Java, but after the Napoleonic Wars, Java became a British territory, which now had a monopoly on the opium import to China.

Britain was a major importer of Chinese goods, such as silk, tea, and porcelain. During the 18th and 19th centuries, the demand for Chinese goods increased significantly, and trade with Britain became one of the main sources to fill the Chinese treasury with silver. In order to reduce the trade deficit caused by Chinese manufacturers, Britain decided to countertrade opium to China. With this intention, the production of opium within the British colonies increased. When the East India Trading Company confirmed its control over India, Britain increased its export of Indian opium to China in 1781.

Britain inherited the opium industry from the failing Mughal Empire, who had a monopoly on opium trade within the country. However, the British government saw opium only as a product for export. Produced in Bengal and the plantations of the Indus-Ganga Plain, opium found its way inside India as well as outside. The East India Trading Company never directly farmed or sold opium. Instead, they came up with a set of laws that allowed opium to travel through the ports they owned, thus collecting the taxes from it. But that wasn't the only way the company earned a profit through opium. One of the laws said that all raw opium had to be sold to the company at a fixed price. The purchased opium was then refined, and the company would sell it at the special auctions they organized.

At first, the Qing dynasty tolerated the importation of opium by the British. They paid in the much-needed silver after all. That same silver would also later be used to buy Chinese tea for the British market, which would mean that silver stayed in the country. The monopoly on tea also allowed the Chinese administration to impose even more taxes on their own subjects in order to fill the royal treasury even faster.

However, it didn't take long for the use of opium by the Chinese citizens to start growing out of control. Opium affected all social classes of the country, rich and poor, soldiers and officers. From Canton Harbor, the use of opium started spreading to the west and north of the country, which led to the Qing emperor issuing an edict against the use of the drug in 1780. But the addiction took its toll on the citizens, and the government had to implement a total ban on opium in 1796. In 1799, the governor of Canton ordered a complete stop to the trade. In order to circumvent this opium trade ban, the merchants converted some of their larger ships into floating warehouses, which they would anchor off the shores of China. Chinese opium dealers would buy the goods from these ship-warehouses and transport them into China on their smaller, faster boats. Setting up this smuggling system allowed foreign merchants to continue legally trading with China while profiting from illegal opium at the same time.

When American merchants joined in smuggling opium, the competition they posed to the British company drove the prices down. Lower prices led to an increased usage of opium, and addiction was once again spreading throughout the country. The demand for opium grew incredibly fast, and soon, the Chinese dealers were searching for more suppliers. Just when the Qing Empire had to deal with the White Lotus Rebellion, the income of silver stopped. The royal treasury started losing money, as Chinese dealers paid for opium in silver. The demand for opium was such that China could not sell enough of their own goods to maintain the profits and for silver to remain in the country.

The Qing officials were considering how to stop the trade of opium, but the main obstacle was the corrupted Chinese officials who profited from the narcotics sale. They even allowed some of the European merchants to gain influence in Canton, and they would navigate the political scene of the city, opening more ways of smuggling opium into China.

A significant change in trade only came in 1834 when the East India Trading Company lost its monopoly in Britain and a reform for free trade took place. Trade with China was then opened to private entrepreneurs, who joined the opium smuggling. Lord William John Napier was sent to China as a superintendent of the British trade, and he had orders to strictly obey Chinese laws and traditions. However, as soon as he came to Canton, he sent a message to the viceroy, regardless of the law that prohibited direct contact with Chinese officials. The Canton viceroy was outraged by this act and issued an edict that temporarily stopped all trade with Britain. In order to show off his power, Napier ordered the British Royal Navy vessels to bombard the fortifications on the banks of Pearl River. All-out war was only avoided due to Napier's illness at the time, but Chinese officials ordered all British merchants to go back to Macau and leave Canton for good.

In 1838, Chinese officials finally began to hunt down and sentence to death opium smugglers and dealers. The following year, the Daoguang Emperor tasked a scholar, Lin Zexu, with eradicating the opium trade with China. Lin wrote a direct letter to Queen Victoria, asking why Britain encouraged its merchants to trade in a drug abroad while at the same time banning the same drug from their own country. Whether the letter ever reached the queen is unknown, but Lin never received an answer. His next step was to close the channel of Pearl River and trap foreign merchants in Canton without the means of transporting their goods deeper into China. He seized and destroyed all opium in Canton, as well as from all foreign ships near Chinese shores.

The new superintendent of British trade, Charles Elliot, ordered all British ships carrying opium to flee and prepare for an upcoming battle. In order to stop other foreign merchants from doing something similar, Lin besieged the foreign district of Canton and trapped them all, making it impossible for them to communicate with their ships. Lin officially banned the opium trade and forbade foreign merchants and Chinese officials from importing opium in China under the threat of a death sentence. However, that didn't stop the black market from flourishing. Instead of bringing opium to Canton, the merchants would unload their cargo on Lintin Island, where the smugglers would pick them up and bring them to mainland China.

Due to an incident in 1839, where a group of British sailors beat up a Japanese villager, Lin Zexu issued an edict that prevented the sale of food to the British. A rumor was then spread that Chinese officials had poisoned the water intended for resupplying the foreign ships. On top of this, a British opium merchant was attacked by pirates, but rumor had it that it was actually attacked by Chinese soldiers instead. By August 24th, Elliot ordered all British ships to leave the shores of China. Over 60 British ships and 2,000 men were stationed in waters outside of China's control. Without any food and water, they were forced to trade with local villagers near the city of Kowloon. However, the Chinese officials in Kowloon banned their people from selling goods to the British. This action caused Elliot to prepare for an attack.

The British ships opened fire on the Chinese vessels. The Chinese returned fire from their own vessels and from the shore. It was only the approach of night that ended the battle. However, with the aid of corrupted Chinese officials, the British managed to buy some provisions. The commander of the army in Kowloon declared a victory when sending reports to the government, in which he greatly underestimated the power of the British Royal Navy.

In October of 1839, a fight between the British ships in Chinese waters was reported. Some merchants who did not trade in opium wanted to sign a bond offered by Lin Zexu, which served as a promise stating that they would not trade or smuggle drugs. Elliot did not approve, and in order to prevent these merchants from entering Canton, he opened fire on the *Royal Saxon*, one of the British merchant ships. The Chinese officials sent help in order to save the *Royal Saxon*, and the battle started. The result of the battle was the destruction of four Chinese war junks (a type of Chinese sailing vessel), followed by the withdrawal of both the British and Chinese fleets. On January 14th, 1840, the Daoguang Emperor ordered all foreign merchants to stop supplying British ships.

While the Chinese officials thought they finally expelled Britain from their lands, the British Parliament was preparing for war. They ordered the East India Trading Company to mobilize all available military forces from India to China. To collect an even larger army, Britain recruited men from all over the British Isles, as well as from the British colonies. The meeting point for all the British forces was Singapore, and they started arriving there by June 1840.

Admiral Guan Tianpei was in charge of the Chinese naval forces. He had experience fighting the British soldiers at the First Battle of Chuenpi. The coastal army was under the command of General Yang Fang, but the Daoguang Emperor and his court had the ultimate command over all the Chinese forces. On the British side, Commodore James Gordon Bremer was in charge of the Royal Marines, and Major General Hugh Gough was in charge of the land forces. The overall command of the forces came from London, where Foreign Secretary Lord Palmerston dictated all actions to be made regarding China.

The war started in June 1840 when Britain gave the ultimatum to the Qing emperor to compensate them for interrupting their trade and the destruction of opium. When the Chinese authorities declined, British soldiers launched an attack on the Chusan Archipelago. The primary target of the attack was Zhoushan Island, where the British planned to start their own trade center on the Chinese coast and rid themselves of Canton dependency. After an intense bombardment from the sea, the British captured the city and port of Dinghai.

The British forces divided their army, and while one fleet was fighting around the Pearl River, the second fleet was sent to the Yellow Sea. In 1841, a direct attack on Canton was planned, and reinforcements from India had just arrived. However, Macau was the first target, and the Qing forces were defeated easily, as they had no counter for the iron, steam-powered warship *Nemesis*. The Chinese junks were old sailing ships developed during the Song dynasty (10th–13th century). The citizens of Macau gave their support to Britain and expelled some of the Qing officials from the city. With this victory, Britain finally had access to a functioning port in southern China. British commanders agreed that taking control of Canton and the Pearl River would place them in a strong position to continue negotiations with the Daoguang Emperor.

Suspecting the British forces would push up the Pearl River to Canton, Qing Admiral Guan Tianpei secured his position in the Humen, a narrow strait in the Pearl River Delta. He reinforced the garrison with 3,000 soldiers and 306 cannons. The British fleet attacked Chuenpi once more and won a decisive victory, capturing the Humen fort, thus forcing the Chinese navy to retreat upriver.

On January 21st, Charles Elliot and the new Chinese Imperial Commissioner Qishan drafted the Convention of Chuenpi in hopes of preventing further conflict. The document allowed equal diplomatic rights for both parties. It secured the exchange of Hong Kong Island and allowed British prisoners to return home unharmed. The convention also stated that Canton must be open for trade by February 1841 and that China had to pay compensation to Britain for the opium that was destroyed in 1838. However, the status of opium as an illegal drug in China was not changed, leaving it an issue to be resolved later. Qishan was arrested for signing this convention without the emperor's permission, but the British government also refused to sign the document. Elliot was recalled from his post, and so, the battle between the British and Chinese forces resumed.

On February 26th, the British forces captured the remaining fortifications in Bogue and moved their fleet closer to Canton, but the city was defended by General Yang Fang and 30,000 men. The shallow rafts of the British ships allowed them to approach Canton from the side, which was considered to be impossible to the Chinese, as the water there was only six feet deep.

The British attacked Canton on March 18th. The city was besieged, and a truce was called for on March 20th. Elliot called off the British navy, ordering the warships to retreat to the Humen. In April, the emperor's cousin and new viceroy Yishan arrived in Canton. He had orders to drive the British out of China completely and to retake the island of Hong Kong. Yishan started reinforcing the city and gathering an army around it. These preparations seeded doubt in the good intentions of the Qing authorities, and civilians started leaving Canton. On May 21st, China launched its first attack on the British Army. The Qing army even used simple fishing boats armed with matchlocks to fight the British Royal Navy. Major General Gough suspected that the Qing planned an attack and sent reinforcements to Canton instead of keeping his fleet at Whampoa as previously planned. These reinforcements arrived at Canton on May 25th and started bombarding the city. The Qing soldiers panicked, and the army dispersed in retreat. By May 30th, 1841, the British had full control of Canton.

Henry Pottinger was sent to China to replace Charles Elliot as superintendent. He arrived in Hong Kong on August 10th and immediately pushed for the continuation of the war and placed pressure on Peking (today's Beijing). On August 25th, the British fleet arrived in Amoy, but the city was already ready for defense. A British combined naval and ground attack on the city was carried out, and they managed to capture it in two days. However, as soon as the Royal Navy retreated to plan further actions, the Qing forces came back to Amoy and proclaimed victory.

Major General Gough sought to advance into China's interior, and he started the campaign of the Yangtze River. In May, Royal Navy ships sailed up the river and captured the emperor's tax barges, which turned out to be a devastating blow to Beijing. In June, the British captured the towns of Wusong and Baoshan, advancing into the Chinese interior. On June 19th, 1842, they occupied the undefended outskirts of Shanghai. By July 14th, the British forces were on the move again, sailing up the Yangtze River and planning to capture the logistically important city of Zhenjiang. The city was devastated. The Chinese army emerged from the city and began what's known as the Battle of Chinkiang. The British soldiers fought off this attack and entered the city. Many Chinese families committed suicide to avoid being imprisoned by the British.

Arriving in Jiangning District on August 9th, the British asked to enter into negotiations, and the city officials agreed, even though they had no permission from Beijing to start peace talks. The British insisted that the treaty be signed by the emperor himself, but as they were unable to comply, the Chinese local administration tried to prolong the negotiations as long as possible. Finally, on August 21st, word came that the Daoguang Emperor was giving authorization to the Chinese diplomats to sign the treaty.

The First Opium War officially ended when the Treaty of Nanking was signed by both the British and Chinese diplomats on August 29th, 1842. The treaty abolished the monopoly on trade that Canton had. Another four ports were opened for foreign trade in China, and China had to pay 21 million silver dollars as war reparations in installments over the next three years. The Qing emperor also agreed to give Hong Kong to Britain in order to colonize it, with Pottinger as its first governor.

Chapter 6 – The Second Opium War

The Treaty of Nanking failed to satisfy British trade requirements, and it also failed to improve the diplomatic relations between the two countries. In 1850, seeing how France and America opened renegotiations of the Treaty of Huangpu and the Treaty of Wangxia with China, Britain demanded that the Chinese authorities renegotiated the Treaty of Nanking. The treaties France and America had with the Qing dynasty had a clause that would allow it to be renegotiated after twelve years. The Treaty of Nanking had no such clause, but Britain called on their "most-favored-nation" status. The most-favored-nation status allowed them to demand equal trade advantages like France and America had. The British demanded that China open all of its territories for trade with British merchants, the legalization of the opium trade, an end to piracy, the admission of a British ambassador in Beijing, and for the English language to be the main language of all future treaties.

In October 1856, a ship under the name *Arrow* was seized by Chinese authorities in Canton under the suspicion of piracy. The *Arrow* used to be a pirate ship, but it was captured and resold to Britain with expired registration forms. Angered by the arrest of the crew from the *Arrow*, British consul Harry Parkes ordered an attack on Canton. The attack started on October 23rd, and the British Army destroyed four forts. Soon after, the British made a demand to be allowed into the city, and when the Chinese refused, they started bombarding the city every ten minutes. The imperial commissioner and Viceroy of Liangguang Ye Mingchen placed a bounty on every British head. On October 29th, the Canton walls were breached, and the British Army entered the city. The exchange of fire continued, with short pauses due to attempts of negotiations. On January 5th, 1857, the British returned to Hong Kong, as the Parliament had decided that their actions during the *Arrow* incident were illegal.

Britain asked America and Russia to join in on their attacks on China, but they refused. However, France joined because of the outrage over the execution of one of their missionaries, Father Auguste Chapdelaine, who crossed the forbidden territory of the Guangxi province.

Canton was once again captured by the British on January 1st, 1858. The delay in fighting was caused by the Indian Rebellion in 1857. Unsatisfied with the development of the *Arrow* situation, the British navy attacked. First, they captured a fort near Canton, meeting almost no resistance. The city fell, and Viceroy Ye Mingchen was arrested and exiled to Calcutta, where he went on a hunger strike until he died.

In May 1858, the French-British coalition moved to capture the Taku Forts, located near today's Tianjin. They held it only for a short time because a peace treaty was soon signed, ending the first phase of the Second Opium War. Even though the US was officially neutral during the Second Opium War, the French and British armies had help from the USS *San Jacinto*, a frigate of the US Navy that assisted them in taking the Taku Forts. The Treaty of Tianjin was signed in June 1858 with Britain, France, Russia, and the US as the signatory parties. At first, the Chinese emperor refused to ratify the treaty but eventually agreed and opened eleven more ports to foreign trade. This treaty allowed Britain, France, Russia, and the US to open embassies in Peking (Beijing), which was a closed city at the time. The Yangtze River was also to be opened for all foreign vessels, and foreigners were to be allowed to travel in China's interior. Finally, China was to pay another war indemnity of six million silver dollars to Britain and France. But the Xianfeng Emperor, who took over the throne in 1850, decided to refuse the foreigners' access to inner China and ordered his Mongol general, Sengge Rinchen, to block the way up the Hai River by guarding the Taku Forts.

In June 1859, a British envoy was escorting new British and French staff for the embassies in Beijing when they were denied passage beyond the Taku forts. The second battle for the forts then took place, and Britain sent 2,200 troops on 21 ships to help with the conflict. The command was given to Admiral Sir James Hope, who sailed from Shanghai to Tianjin. Sengge Rinchen wanted to let the envoy with embassy officials pass, but they had to continue without any military escort. The British refused to comply, and they attacked the Taku forts by blowing up the obstacles that were blocking their path. Sengge Rinchen ordered fire on the British vessels and sank four gunboats while damaging two more. The US Navy was planning on maintaining their neutrality, but American Commodore Josiah Tattnall decided to support the British navy anyway. He provided cover fire, protecting the British retreat. China's victory at Taku served as inspiration for resisting against the foreigners.

In the summer of 1860, the Third Battle of Taku Forts took place. The British troops attacking the fort counted 11,000, and leading them was Lieutenant-General James Hope. Once again, France helped them by sending 6,700 troops under the command of Lieutenant-General Charles Cousin-Montauban. Altogether, they had 173 ships. Amongst their ranks, the British had Chinese supporters from the south, who were eager to break away from the Qing dynasty and help the foreigners. The coalition forces captured the cities of Yantai and Dalian, thus sealing the Bohai Gulf. They decided to land near Beitang, which was around 1.9 miles from the

Taku forts. After three weeks of besieging the forts, they were finally captured on August 21st.

Tianjin was captured three days later, and the Anglo-French army started their march toward Beijing. The Xianfeng Emperor considered peace and sent his diplomats to negotiate, but British diplomat Harry Parkes insulted the emperor's emissary. In addition, the rumor of the prefect of Tianjin being kidnapped by the British started spreading. So, instead of peace talks, Harry Parkes was arrested, tortured, and interrogated. Half of his men were executed, while the other half had to suffer torture by "slow slicing." The unrecognizable bodies were then returned to the British leadership, who were, of course, infuriated.

On September 18th, 1860, the combined Anglo-French army launched a full-scale attack on the Chinese troops. The battle took place at Zhangjiawan, a town to the east of the Tongzhou district of Beijing. The British cavalry crushed the Mongolians, while the French infantry dealt with the Chinese troops. The combined Anglo-French artillery provided cover and inflicted massive losses on the Chinese army.

The Anglo-French army continued to march toward Beijing but was stopped by Sengge Rinchen, who led the Qing infantry and Mongolian cavalry. The armies clashed on September 20th in front of a canal that connects Beijing with the Peiho River. The battle took place in the vicinity of the Palikao Bridge and is known by the name of the Battle of Palikao. The Qing troops found themselves trapped by the canal and unable to retreat, and the Chinese suffered massive losses. Several frontal attacks of the Anglo-French army completely obliterated the infantry led by Sengge Rinchen, as well as his Mongolian cavalry.

The Battle of Palikao

https://en.wikipedia.org/wiki/Second_Opium_War#/media/File:La_bataille_de_Pa likiao.jpg

The Xianfeng Emperor placed his brother, Prince Gong, in charge of the negotiations that centered on the prisoners. The British demanded all prisoners be released, but China couldn't accept these terms. This provoked Britain, and they ordered an attack on Beijing. The attack on the city walls started on October 11th. The Anglo-French army was ready to enter the city and fight, but at 11:30 on the same evening, the gates opened, and the city surrendered. The Xianfeng Emperor already fled the capital. First, he went to the Chengde Summer Palace and then to the Rehe province. Britain considered destroying the entirety of the Forbidden City but satisfied themselves with burning only the Summer Palace (Yiheyuan) and the Old Summer Palace (Yuanmingyuan). All the British prisoners were released, but some of them were completely unrecognizable due to the inflicted torture. The bodies of the prisoners who did not survive were also retrieved.

The Treaty of Tianjin, which had been signed in 1858, was finally ratified by the emperor's brother, Prince Gong, at the Convention of

Peking, which took place on October 18th, 1860. The ratification of this treaty concluded the Second Opium War.

The British, French, and Russians were given permission to establish a permanent diplomatic presence in Beijing. The Chinese also agreed to pay all the war indemnities previously stated by the treaty. Britain was given the Kowloon Peninsula, located right next to Hong Kong. Furthermore, Christian missionaries gained full civil rights, which meant they were now able to own property in China and to freely spread their religion. The trade of opium was also legalized by this treaty.

British Prime Minister William Ewart Gladstone later condemned the Opium Wars and denounced the British violence toward China. Gladstone criticized the Opium Wars as unjust and disgraceful, as Britain's morality was in question since they had imposed a free narcotics trade on one country while keeping it illegal in their own. His hostility toward the opium trade originated in the fact that his own sister was an opium addict.

Chapter 7 – Taiping Rebellion

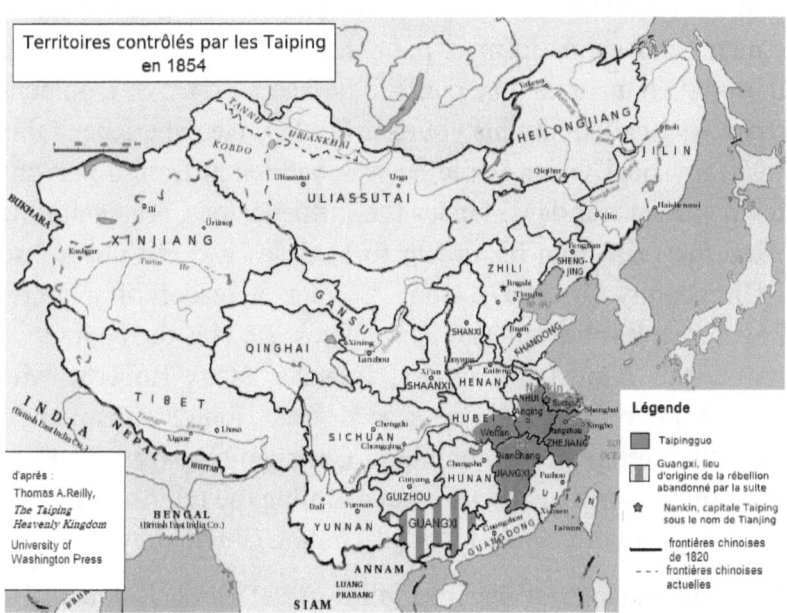

Area under the control of the Taiping Heavenly Kingdom in red

https://en.wikipedia.org/wiki/Taiping_Rebellion

Between 1850 and 1864, China was torn apart not just by the Opium Wars against the British Empire; it was also torn apart due to an internal struggle known as the Taiping Rebellion, or the Taiping

Civil War. The fighting started between the Qing dynasty and the Taiping Heavenly Kingdom.

China suffered greatly after the First Opium War. It also suffered natural disasters and economic problems due to a severe lack of silver, which caused the national poverty level to rise. The population of China doubled during this period of time, but the amount of agricultural land stayed the same. Famine was widespread, and the corrupt Manchu government didn't do anything to resolve it. The southern provinces of China, inhabited by the Hakka Chinese people, were one of the strongest voices against the Manchu.

The Taiping Heavenly Kingdom was founded by a charismatic Hakka man who came from a poor southern village. He called himself Hong Xiuquan, and he claimed he had a dream of a golden-haired man who called him his younger brother. He experienced this dream as a mystical vision while he was bedridden from a nervous breakdown for several days. Under the influence of Christianity, he recognized the man from his dream to be Jesus and felt obliged to spread Christianity. In 1847, Hong became a leader of a secret society with many followers and apprentices. He was the apprentice of an American Baptist missionary, Issachar Jacox Roberts, who refused to baptize Hong, as he saw it was Hong's intention to politicize the religion. Combining Christianity with Taoism, Confucianism, and Millenarianism but claiming the rebirth of the old Chinese Shang Di faith, Hong founded Taiping Christianity.

Feng Yunshan was one of the first followers of Hong Xiuquan. He was a village teacher in a village in Hua County. He was also of Hakka descent, and together with Hong, he preached the Taiping version of Christianity. Deep in the Thistle Mountains, Feng organized a group of followers into a society under the name "God Worshipping Society." Feng became the strategist and the administrator of the rebellion, and Hong Xiuquan bestowed the title of "South King" upon him.

Taiping Christianity had two other prominent leaders who claimed they had the right to speak to God and Jesus. Yang Xiuqing claimed he was deaf and mute before he was introduced into the God Worshipping Society and that he regained his ability to hear and speak at one of the Society's meetings. He also claimed he could enter a trance that would allow him to speak directly to God. Hong and Feng investigated the claims of Yang Xiuqing and declared them to be genuine. He participated in the Taiping Rebellion from the start and rose in the ranks of the rebels quickly. He was promoted to commander of the rebel army by Hong himself, even though he had no military experience, and he was given the title of "East King."

Xiao Chaogui was a farmer from Wuxuan known for his strength and valor. He became the leader of his region and claimed he could speak directly to Jesus. He was also married to Yang Yunijao, who claimed she visited heaven during her illness, where she was told that a new religious instructor was coming. She recognized Hong Xiuquan to be this instructor. Xiao Chaogui was given the title of "West King," and he became one of the principal commanders of the Taiping army.

This sect grew in power and was never recognized as an official religion in China. Like other secret societies, it was persecuted by the Qing authorities. The followers of Taiping Christianity fought piracy and bandits, protecting their homes. But they had to act as a guerilla force due to the constant persecution they faced. This guerrilla army eventually grew into a massive rebellion.

On January 11th, 1851, on his birthday, Hong Xiuquan proclaimed that he was the "Heavenly King," thus starting a new dynasty known as the Taiping Heavenly Kingdom. Their mission was to overthrow the ruling Qing dynasty, as they had lost the Mandate of Heaven, or so Hong claimed. The first uprising that marked the beginning of the Taiping Rebellion was named after the rebel base in Jintian, located in the Guangxi province. The rebels were recognizable for undoing their Manchu queues. They also changed their garments and tied a red cloth around their heads.

The Taiping armies started marching toward Dahuangjiangkou, where they prepared for an attack. The Qing forces, under the command of General Xiang Rong, counted around 3,000 men when they tried to attack the rebels. He was soon joined by the imperial army, which was led by General Li Nengchen, and they attacked Dahuangjiangkou simultaneously from the east and west. However, the imperial armies found themselves in the middle of a minefield that had been set up by the rebels, and they were forced to change their tactics. During the night, the rebel forces escaped and retreated to Wuxuan County of the Guangxi province. They were followed by the imperial army, and the two clashed soon after near Sanli Dyke, with the short battle ending in a stalemate. Xiang Rong gathered an army of 6,000 men to attack the rebels, but they managed to drive them back. At the battle of Du'ao Ridge, the rebels were victorious in defeating the imperial army, but they could not progress north, as Xiang Rong and his troops were blocking the path. So instead, the rebels started recruiting people from nearby villages. They continued to grow in numbers and managed to obtain a large number of supplies, as they had the support of the majority of commoners.

Finally, the rebel forces defeated the imperial army in the Guangxi province and reached the neighboring Hunan province. However, the delayed advance of the Taiping forces gave the Qing army an opportunity to reinforce the city of Changsha, the capital of Hunan province, which was the goal of the rebels. The Taiping rebels' first attempt at doing so cost them over 10,000 men, which they lost in an ambush near the Xiang River.

The rebels then decided to recruit local miners and order them to build siege tunnels, which would help them breach the city walls. While the tunnels were being dug, the rebels took control of the surrounding areas of Changsha. In order to boost the morale of his armies, Xiao Chaogui donned the royal robes with the intention to fight while wearing them. He also hoisted a large banner above his head, but he was easily spotted by Qing gunners and was wounded by a cannonball. In September of 1852, Xiao Chaogui, the West

King, succumbed to his wounds. Hong Xiuquan called off the siege since his friend, and one of the main commanders of the army, had died. The Taiping forces left Changsha and continued north toward Wuchang.

The Taiping forces moved slowly toward Wuchang, as they had to perform deceptive maneuvers to lose the pursuit of the Qing imperial army. They destroyed the bridges behind them, abandoned their boats, and resumed the path on foot, just to continue by boat as soon as they reached a village or town on the riverbank. They also used pontoon bridges to cross the river and hired boatmen to regularly check on the advancement of the Qing troops. By December 1852, the rebels reached Dongting Lake, where they occupied the city of Yueyang. Instead of directly attacking Wuchang, the commanders of the rebel army decided to first take the undefended commercial towns of Hanyang and Hankou. The Taiping forces built two floating bridges by linking boats together over the Yangtze River to connect these towns, with Wuchang on its northern side, where the defense was weaker.

The governor of the Hubei province, who resided in the capital of Wuchang, ordered all houses outside of the city walls to be destroyed in order for the gunners to have a clear path to fire. In addition, he promised that all citizens of Wuchang would receive a bounty for Taiping heads, namely twenty silver for a head with long hair, as that would represent a rebel veteran, and ten silver for the shorthaired rebels because that would signify newer recruits. However, the citizens were angered by the destruction of their homes and showed sympathy for the Taiping rebels. The city was besieged for twenty days. The Qing forces within the city blocked the gates with the earth and debris of the destroyed houses, and they created listening posts along the city walls to pinpoint the tunneling that would breach the city. Their measures proved to be ineffective, though, as Wuchang fell on January 12th, 1853.

After taking over Wuchang, the Taiping rebels decided not to march directly to Beijing as they had heard rumors of a large Qing army to the north. Instead, they opted to go east along the Yangtze River and take over Nanjing, where they would set up a base for further actions in northern China.

However, Wuchang was recaptured by the imperial forces in 1854. It would soon be lost once again. The Qing army would regain control of the city again on December 19th, 1856, this time permanently.

The Taiping forces captured Nanjing (Nanking) on March 19th, 1853. Hong Xiuquan established it as the capital city of the Heavenly Kingdom, changing its name to Tianjing (Heavenly Capital). The Manchus were the enemies of the Taiping, and the rebels regarded them as demons. So, all Manchu men were slaughtered inside the city, while the women were forced beyond the city walls to be burned alive. The rebels destroyed most of the imperial buildings built during the Qing and Ming dynasties. One of the prominent buildings that was destroyed was the Porcelain Tower of Nanjing, a royal pagoda built in the 15th century. This tower was noted by many European explorers as one of the Seven Wonders of the World. Shortly after conquering Nanjing, however, the Taiping commanders launched two new military expeditions, one in the north and one in the west. The northern campaign was a complete failure, but the western one was somewhat successful as it gained some territories for the rebels.

Hong Xiuquan decided to start ruling through written proclamations only and thus modeled his policies and administration based on the previous emperors of China. He lived in luxury, indulging himself with women who lived in his inner chambers. Disappointed in Hong's impractical policies, Yang Xiuqing challenged his leader's commands. Hong Xiuquan became suspicious of Yang's motives and his vast network of spies. Soon after, Hong gave orders to Wei Changhui and Qin Rigang, the military leaders he most trusted, to slaughter Yang and all of his followers. Wei and Qin complied, but their ultimate goal was to actually get rid of Hong Xiuquan. Hong heard about their plans and immediately issued the arrest and execution of both commanders. These events are known as the Tianjing Incident of 1856.

The remaining leaders of the Taiping army tried to persuade the Europeans to join their fight against the Qing dynasty. The Europeans claimed to be neutral, although some military advisors were openly working for the Qing emperor. The Taiping forces started losing popularity amongst the Chinese citizens, who were repelled by their hostility toward Chinese customs and Confucianism. The middle and upper classes of Chinese society started siding with the Qing dynasty.

In the Hunan province, Zeng Guofan raised and organized the Xiang Army. Zeng was a statesman, scholar, and military general who gathered regional and local militia in order to fight off the Taiping rebels. His army was financed by local nobles and members of high society, who were opposed to the Manchu-led imperial army, which was financed directly from the royal treasury. The Xiang Army first recovered Changsha, the capital of the Hunan province. Soon after, he managed to recapture Wuchang and Hanyang. For these victories, he was awarded the title of vice president of the Board of War. The Qing leadership started using Zeng's army instead of their own troops, seeing the success this new army had. By September 1858, the Xiang Army gained control over the whole Jiangxi province.

The Taiping forces defeated the imperial army that was besieging Nanjing in 1860 and started their move to expand the borders of the Heavenly Kingdom. In March of the same year, the rebels took Hangzhou. In May, Changzhou fell and in June Suzhou.

In June 1861, under the command of Lai Wenguang, the Taiping forces occupied Shanghai and managed to hold it for five months before abandoning it. They had to withdraw from the city due to the constant threat from the Qing forces. But by March 1862, the Taiping leader Li Xiucheng had gathered an army of over 600,000 men. Shanghai was an important city as it was isolated, easy to defend, and had an international port, and it was to be the next target.

The first to attack were the Taiping forces, which were commanded by Li Rongfa, who led the invasion with 20,000 men on March 1st, 1862. They occupied one whole district of the city, which was only defended by the Green Standard Army. Their commander, Huang Yisheng, requested help from the British and French, but they wanted to remain neutral. Instead, help came from the American mercenary commander Frederick Townsend Ward and his troops.

As a mercenary, Ward was employed by imperial authorities to organize the Shanghai Foreign Arms Corps. Recruiting Westerners, sober or otherwise, Ward couldn't organize an army that would be willing to fight alongside the Chinese. His army was defeated in battle at Chingpu in 1861, but the battle did form the nucleus for what would later become known as the "Ever Victorious Army." By the summer of 1861, a training camp for Ward was set up, where he trained the Chinese in gunnery, tactics, drills, customs, and ceremonies of both the Western and Chinese armies. The Chinese soldiers trained by Ward were able to respond to Western verbal, as well as non-verbal, commands. They wore Western-style uniforms for which they were often mocked. Later, when the Ever Victorious Army gained prestige, those uniforms became a symbol of pride. These troops were financed both by the government and from the private funds of nobles. It was important to pay these troops well as compensation for not looting. Ward strictly forbade looting in order to keep the locals supporting his troops.

Ward's army achieved victories in every encounter they had with the Taiping forces. In fact, they were so efficient in their endeavors that by March 1862, the Qing government officially named them the Ever Victorious Army, and this is how they are still known to history. Ward himself was made a 4th-rank and then a 3rd-rank mandarin, which was the highest title the Manchu administration had for foreigners or "barbarians."

On April 10th, 1862, Ward led his army to recapture Shanghai. Fighting side by side with the troops of the Green Standard Army, the districts of Shanghai fell one by one. On May 1st, the Taiping forces under Li Rongfa surrendered to the Ever Victorious Army in Shanghai's district of Nanhui. The Qing government had full control over the eastern and southern Shanghai districts by this point. Rongfa had to retreat to Pudong with his army. However, the battles for the districts continued throughout May until there were no more Taiping forces in a radius of thirty miles around Shanghai.

In September of 1862, the Taiping army tried to regain Shanghai once more. They sent 80,000 men under the command of Tan Shaoguang, but they were defeated by the Qing defenders. The Taiping commanders ordered another attack shortly after, this time sending 70,000 men who moved very quickly and managed to surprise the defenders enough to get close to the city. The Qing fleet attacked the Taiping forces from the river, however, and managed to gain some ground. Support came from the Ever Victorious Army, and the rebels were finally forced to retreat. The Taiping army tried to break through Shanghai's defenses four more times until Hong Xiuquan finally called off all attacks, thus ending the conflict over the city.

After freeing Shanghai, Frederick Townsend Ward led his army to the north of the Zhejiang province. Together with other British and French troops, he helped free the city of Cixi from the Taiping rebel forces. Here, Ward was mortally wounded after receiving a bullet in his abdomen. He lived for one day before succumbing to his wound, but not before making sure he wrote a will in which his Chinese wife and his brother and sister would be secured. The command of the Ever Victorious Army was passed to Major General Charles George Gordon, who continued the string of victories. For his deeds against the Taiping rebels, he received honors from both the Tongzhi Emperor, who took the throne in 1861, and from the British government. People gave him the nickname "Chinese Gordon."

At this time, in the Sichuan province, Shi Dakai, one of the Taiping Rebellion leaders and a poet, had been operating for over six years. He was also known as Wing King, "Lord of Five Thousand Years," and is often mentioned in myths and legends due to his martial skills and sense of justice. In December 1862, he tried to lead his troops across the Jinsha River but was constantly under heavy fire from the Qing forces and had to retreat. The river also flooded, so it wasn't easy to cross. After several attempts, with his troops running out of rations and the Qing imperial army closing in on them, Shi Dakai decided to make a deal. He negotiated with the Qing officer to spare the lives of his men if he would turn himself over. Shi Dakai was arrested and executed by slow slicing. Out of the 6,000 men who accompanied him, 4,000 were released as promised.

The Qing army was reorganized, and the command over it was given to Zeng Guofan, Zuo Zongtang, and Li Hongzhang. They were all statesmen and military generals, and some of them later became diplomats. They began the reconquest of all the territories taken by the Taiping rebels, and by 1864, they managed to retake almost all of them.

In 1860, Zeng Guofan became the viceroy of Liangjiang and took the opportunity this title gave him to retake Nanjing. By 1863, the entire area around the city was freed from the rebels after a series of battles. The Third Battle of Nanking (Nanjing) started on March 14th, 1864, when Zeng Guoquan, the younger brother of Zeng Guofan, attacked the city using ladders to climb its walls. The defenders were able to beat the Qing forces, thus pushing them to change their tactics. They started digging tunnels at the gates of Nanjing, but the defenders dug their own tunnels to counter them and built a second wall to secure the city. On July 3rd, the Qing forces managed to take over the Purple Mountains and its Dibao Castle. This strategically excellent location provided several dozen artillery positions, and so, the bombardment of Nanjing commenced. Two weeks later, on July 19th, the city wall collapsed due to the tunnel explosives that were placed under the Taiping Gates. The attackers rushed inside the city on four fronts.

The central front was led by imperial General Li Chendian. His task was to lead the attack toward the palace, where Hong Xiuquan used to reside. The right front was led by imperial General Liu Lianjie.

His troop's task was to push toward the Shence gate, where they would meet the force entering the city by ladders. Together, their task was to lead the attack on the Lion Mountain and to take Yifeng Gate. The central left, which was led by imperial General Peng Yuju, had the task of attacking the Tongji Gate. And finally, the left front, under the command of imperial General Xiao Fusi, attacked the Chaoyang and Hongwu gates.

The rebels put up a fierce fight, but they were no match for 60,000 imperial soldiers. They did hope to repel the attackers beyond the city gates, but their morale was at an all-time low after witnessing the fall of the Chaoyang gate. By evening, all the Nanjing gates were in the hands of the imperial Qing forces. However, Li Xiucheng managed to escape the city with the son of Hong Xiuquan, and together, they fled toward Qingliang Mountain. Zeng Guoquan sent a cavalry unit to pursue them, and Li got separated from Hong's son. Li was captured on July 22nd, 1864, but he wasn't executed until August. Many Taiping leaders and generals were executed after the fall of Nanjing; only Lai Wenguang managed to escape with his 3,000 men.

Hong Xiuquan died during the siege of Nanjing. The city was low on food due to the siege, and he ordered his subjects to eat wild plants and medicinal herbs. Hong gathered some weeds from the palace gardens and ate them. As a result, he fell ill in April and died on June 1st, 1864. It is possible that Hong was ill because he ate some poisonous plants, but some historians suggest he committed suicide by poisoning. He was buried according to Taiping customs near the Ming Imperial Palace in Nanjing. His successor was Hong Tianguifu, his teenage son. After the fall of Nanjing, the Qing forces exhumed Hong Xiuquan's body, cut off his head, and burned the remains. As eternal punishment for his rebellion, the ashes of Hong Xiuquan were blasted out of a cannon to make sure he would never have a proper resting place.

Chapter 8 – Self-Strengthening of China

After the Second Opium War, at the time of the Taiping Rebellion, the Self-Strengthening Movement was organized in China. The movement's idea was to use the available Western technology in Asia to preserve the Confucian values of the empire. This is why this movement is also known as the Western Affairs Movement or Westernization. The movement worked on institutional reforms, which lasted from 1861 until 1895.

The term "self-strengthening" is nothing new in China's culture. In fact, it comes directly from the *I Ching* (*Book of Changes*), a divination text, where it is written, "The superior man makes himself strong." This phrase was used before by other dynasties and emperors, each giving it his own interpretation. For example, the Qianlong Emperor wrote that self-strengthening was necessary for repelling foreigners.

Historians are currently dividing the movement into three phases. During the first phase, which lasted from 1861 until 1872, a diplomatic office and a college were established in order to work on the adoption of Western technologies, scientific knowledge, and training techniques. Western newspapers were being translated into

Chinese in order to obtain knowledge about the West. Later, this practice spread to Western books.

The School of Combined Learning, or the Tongwen Guan, was established in 1862 in Beijing. At first, it offered only classes in the English language, and it had ten students and one teacher, a British missionary named John S. Burdon. Astronomy and mathematics were added by 1866. By 1877, the school extended the classes they offered to French, German, Russian, and Japanese, as well as chemistry, machine-making, astronomy, mathematics, medicine, international law, and geography. By then, the school had over a hundred students. Similar language schools were opened in Shanghai (1862), Guangzhou (1863), and Fuzhou (1866).

In April 1861, the Imperial Maritime Customs Service was founded, with a British diplomat Horatio Nelson Lay as the inspector-general. The task of the office was to collect tariffs and generate new revenues from the import of foreign goods. After the Taiping Rebellion, the Chinese officials had lost their authority over the Westerners, and the customs office had to employ a foreigner in this high-ranking position. The Imperial Maritime Customs Service evolved from the previously established system of the Inspectorate of Customs, which was founded in 1854. The office did not bring anything new, but it did institutionalize the previous system. The custom tariffs collected through the Imperial Maritime Customs Service paid off the war indemnities from 1860 that were owed to the British Empire and France. The office also provided the means for financing the opening of Tongwen Guan and other schools, the Fuzhou Navy Yard, and educational mission to America. The Customs Service also built lighthouses and modernized Chinese maritime navigation. Sir Robert Hart became the new inspector-general of the Customs Service in 1863. He tried to get involved with China's Self-Strengthening Movement and offered to reorganize and modernize China's imperial fleet and to open a Chinese post office, but the Qing dynasty wasn't ready to allow foreigners to get involved in the self-strengthening of their nation.

Military modernization was the most important aspect of the Self-Strengthening Movement. China needed to build military arsenals and strengthen their navy by building dockyards. Zeng Guofan and Yung Wing were the ones who established the Shanghai arsenal. Yung Wing was the first Chinese student educated in America (Yale in 1854). The Nanjing and Tianjin arsenals were built by Li Hongzhang. In addition, the Fuzhou Dockyard, where ships were built for the Chinese navy, was founded by Zuo Zongtang. Some of the Westerners were involved in the actual building projects but only as advisors or administrative aid.

The Chinese government was the main sponsor of military industrialization, and that meant its progress was often thwarted by inefficient bureaucracy. The government also found these building projects to be too expensive. The Jiangnan Arsenal built guns, more specifically, Remington-type rifles. The production was so slow, however, that between 1871 and 1873, they only produced 4,200 rifles. They were inferior to the imported Remington rifles and more costly because the production was so slow. The shipbuilding program was no better. It relied on imported materials and foreign expertise, which proved to be more expensive than simply buying British ships. Chinese officials relied on foreign expertise so much that they would even hire people who were not even qualified; just because they were foreign, they were trusted to have sufficient knowledge. Corruption ruled the building sites of everything from the arsenals to dockyards. Plenty of opportunities for corruption arose with the procurement of materials, construction contracts, and distribution of wages.

Another aspect of the military self-strengthening was the complete reorganization of the army. The Green Standard Army was reduced to only a fraction of what it used to be. Those who remained were armed and equipped in the Western-style and were also drilled in Western tactics. In 1862, the Qing court chose 30,000 men of the Eight Banners to be specially trained in the Western military style. This army was named the Peking Field Force.

The first period of self-strengthening ended with riots in Tianjin in 1870 when a number of foreigners were killed. The relations between China and the Western powers became somewhat strained, but the second phase of self-strengthening was initiated anyway. Li Hongzhang became the leader of the new reforms. He is noted for starting and supporting over ninety percent of the projects for the modernization of China.

The second phase of self-strengthening is known for giving special attention to commerce, industry, and agriculture. The main goal was to generate wealth for the country, strengthening it economically. China began developing shipping, railways, the mining sector, and telegraphy, all profit-oriented industries that were supervised by the government. Again, governmental supervision resulted in increased corruption and nepotism, which slowed down progress. Since there was no competition from private owners, the industry prevented economic developments.

Li Hongzhang actively sought to give even more government assistance to Chinese entrepreneurs who were competing against foreign enterprises. As an example, the China Merchants' Steam Navigation Company was extremely effective and gained control over all shipping services. Between 1872 and 1877, the company grew and had to expand from 4 to 29 steamships. This is due to removing all management and capital from government hands and giving them to compradors. Coal and iron mines, as well as textile mills, implemented similar plans and started prospering.

In 1874, under the initiative of Li Hongzhang, schools in Beijing, the Fuzhou Navy Yard, and Kiangnan Arsenal began teaching Western mathematics, believing it to be the core of Western success in technology. Military education also became an important part of China's school system. In 1872, China launched an educational mission to the United States. The prime objective was to enroll Chinese cadets in a US military academy, but in 1881, the academy refused to accept Chinese students. In 1875, cadets from the Fuzhou Navy Yard started enrolling in British and French schools instead.

Upon their return, the students engaged in the foundation of the Beiyang Fleet, the largest modernized fleet in China at that time. Li Hongzhang pointed out the importance of military training, and the government started sending Chinese officers to Germany for further training. Due to his efforts, a naval academy in Tianjin opened in 1880. But it wasn't only foreign military schools that attracted Chinese students. The Chinese government also sent their officials abroad to learn modern science and catch up with the Western world.

The third phase of the Self-Strengthening Movement took place between 1885 and 1895. During this phase, the Navy Board was founded as an effort to further modernize the army. But at this stage, the enthusiasm for self-strengthening started to diminish. The conservative side had a huge influence in the court, and Prince Gong, who was a member of the Grand Council at the time, was overwhelmed and overthrown. Nonetheless, the cotton and textile industries gained favoritism from the imperial court, which heavily invested in their development.

The government started investing in not just the navy but the army as well. Officers were sent to Germany, Great Britain, France, and Japan to study, which would allow them to become the next military leaders of the Chinese army. In 1885, Li Hongzhang opened the Tianjin Military Academy with the assistance of Germany. This academy offered military training, drill surveying, fortification, mathematics, and science taught in the German language, and the program lasted for two years.

In 1898, the Guangxu Emperor and his supporters initiated the Hundred Days' Reform. They planned to enact cultural, political, educational, and national reforms starting on September 22nd. However, due to conservative opponents, the reforms failed after 103 days. These reforms came about after China fought a war with Japan in 1894 and 1895, a war which they lost. This was a hard blow to China, which regarded Japan as inferior due to its size and because it was a tributary state. In order to cover up their shame and to prevent such losses from happening again, a series of reforms took place. In order to follow Western standards, China had to modernize its government and society, not just the military and industries. Japan had already adopted a Western-style government by establishing a parliament by the time the reforms rolled out.

The reforms of the Guangxu Emperor were supposed to:
- Put an end to the old-fashioned examination system.
- Close all sinecures.
- Provide classes of Western liberal arts and Chinese classical arts at Peking University.
- Open schools in all provinces and cities, placing emphasis on agricultural schools.
- Modernize the educational system.
- Enforce capitalism to develop the economy.
- Establish a constitutional monarchy.
- Further modernize the military.
- Open more naval academies.
- Turn unused military lands into farms.
- Industrialize manufacturing and commerce.
- Open trade schools for Chinese goods, such as tea, silk, and traditional crafts.
- Open a bureau for mining and transportation industries.

However, suspicious of foreign plots, the conservatives, who were led by Empress Dowager Cixi, the regent to the throne, and Prince Duan, strongly opposed these reforms. The emperor's supporters plotted to remove Empress Dowager Cixi from power, but their plans were revealed. This led to a coup that ended the Hundred Days' Reform.

Chapter 9 – Empress Dowager Cixi

A photograph of Empress Dowager Cixi

https://en.wikipedia.org/wiki/Empress_Dowager_Cixi

Empress Dowager Cixi was a Chinese empress and regent who held most of the power during the reigns of the Tongzhi and Guangxu Emperors. She was born in Beijing in 1835 to a third-class duke named Huizheng and Lady Fuca. As an adolescent, she was presented in court amongst sixty other candidates to be the consort for the Xianfeng Emperor. Cixi was chosen to stay and was given the sixth rank of consorts as "Noble Lady Lan." In 1854, she rose to the fifth level of consorts and was named "Concubine Yi." Next year, when she became pregnant, she was elevated once more to "Consort Yi." She gave birth to a son, the future Tongzhi Emperor, and when he turned one year old, she was again elevated in status to "Noble Consort Yi," with only Empress Niohuru being her superior.

Cixi was known to be educated, and she was able to read and write Chinese. She also helped the Xianfeng Emperor in his daily state business, as she read for the emperor in his ailing days and often took notes for him. This act gave her the opportunity to learn about governing the Chinese Empire, and she kept herself well informed about state affairs.

The Xianfeng Emperor died in 1861, but before his death, he appointed eight of his ministers to be the regents to his five-year-old son. He also summoned Empress Niohuru and Noble Consort Yi (Cixi), instructing them to cooperate in the upbringing of the future emperor. It is believed that the two women were summoned by the dying emperor in order to give them royal seals that would keep the regent ministers in check. But these seals were informal, and it might be that they were just presents for the emperor's beloved ones. Once the emperor was dead, Empress Niohuru became "Empress Dowager Ci'an," and Noble Consort Yi was elevated to the status "Empress Dowager Cixi." They were also known as the East Empress Dowager and the West Empress Dowager, respectively.

Because she was the lower-ranked empress dowager, she had no real political power. Immediately after the death of the Xianfeng Emperor, she started plotting to seize some power for herself. Her son, even though he was emperor, had no influence over state affairs as he was too young. Cixi became close with some of the court officials, including the Empress Dowager Ci'an. The two of them had become friends as soon as Cixi came to the royal court as a consort. Now, they plotted together to gain power that would be greater than that of the eight regents.

The eight regents did not appreciate their meddling in politics. The confrontation between the two parties became so intense that Empress Dowager Ci'an started refusing to show up to court audiences. Instead, she left all the politics in the hands of Cixi. Cixi started gaining the support of various ministers and court officials and even gained support from Princes Gong and Chun, the Tongzhi Emperor's uncles who were brilliant statesmen. With their support, Empress Dowager Cixi became the de facto ruler by paying attention to the politics behind the curtain.

Soon after, in November 1861, the eight regents were dismissed under accusations that they were guilty of incompetent negotiations with the Western powers that led to the flight of the Xianfeng Emperor to the Rehe province at the end of the Second Opium War. To show her great will and mercy, Empress Dowager Cixi executed only three out of the eight regents, although some sources claim all eight were forced to commit suicide. The leader of the eight regents, Sushun, was beheaded while the other two were given white silk ropes to hang themselves. She refused to execute the families of the regent ministers, breaking imperial protocol.

Also, in November, Empress Dowager Cixi rewarded Prince Gong for his help. He became prince regent, and his daughter was given the rank of princess. As one of the first actions of her de facto rule, Cixi, as well as Ci'an, issued two edicts, with the first giving them absolute decisive power and the second changing the emperor's title from Qixiang ("auspicious") to Tongzhi ("collective stability"). Due to their inexperience in leading the state, the two empresses had to rely on the Grand Council to deal with complex bureaucratic procedures. Both Cixi and Ci'an were the first to receive state documents, and they would then pass them to Prince Gong and the Grand Council. After discussing the issues, the members of the Grand Council would seek an audience with the empresses and draw up imperial orders. The empresses were the only ones who had the royal seal, and they would apply it to all the edicts after carefully reading them.

During the Taiping Rebellion, Empress Dowager Cixi was forced to place the defense of Chinese cities into the hands of the Han Chinese. This was due to the increased decrepit state of the Manchu ethnic group. The most prominent Han general who commanded the Chinese army was Zeng Guofan. After the rebellion, Cixi started appointing Han Chinese as governors of southern provinces, which led to major resentment in the imperial court, as it was still bound to Manchu traditions.

During the Taiping Rebellion, Prince Gong was able to gather support from the Han Chinese armies. He also served as prince regent, as head of the Grand Council, and as a minister of foreign affairs. All of these positions gave him too much power, and Cixi started feeling threatened by him. She quickly accused him of corruption and of showing no respect for the emperor. By April 1865, Cixi had gathered a series of accusations against Prince Gong, and as a result, she stripped him of all of his titles, positions, and offices, although he was allowed to keep his noble status. Pressured by his brothers, Princes Dun and Chun, and other members of the imperial court, Cixi allowed Prince Gong to return to his office as a minister of foreign affairs, but she did not give him back his title of prince regent. Even though he was her most important ally until now, Cixi made sure he would never again have political influence. The demotion of Prince Gong revealed to everyone just how much power the empress actually had.

Empress Dowager Cixi was known for her stubborn traditional mentality. Even though she initially saw the benefits of the Self-Strengthening Movement, she was quick to dismiss novelties if they collided with tradition. For instance, she was against the construction of a railroad in Beijing since the trains were too loud and would disturb the imperial tombs. Once the railroad was finished, in spite of her protests, she asked if it would be possible for the trains to be pulled by horses. She also returned the warships bought from Britain because they were staffed with British sailors under the command of British officers. But most of all, she was afraid of liberal-thinking

Chinese people who studied abroad. She even managed to stop the policy of sending students to foreign countries for studies for some time.

Empress Dowager Ci'an was the one who guided the Tongzhi Emperor to marry Lady Arute when he turned seventeen. Cixi did not agree to this marriage since she was the daughter of one of the eight regents that she had accused and sentenced to death by suicide. Choosing Lady Arute must have been very irritating for Cixi. The other reason for not agreeing with the marriage was that Lady Arute's zodiac sign was a tiger while Cixi's was a goat. As traditional and superstitious as she was, Empress Dowager Cixi interpreted this as a sign that she would fall prey to Lady Arute. While she was welcomed at court with all the honors and grace, Lady Arute was warned to be wary of Cixi and her hatred. She was advised to be humble and docile in Cixi's presence, but Lady Arute replied that she was a noble empress who entered the palace through the front door, while Cixi was just a consort who entered through the back. She was defiant toward Cixi, which instigated even more hatred between the two.

In order to separate the newly wedded couple, Cixi ordered them to spend less time together and instead devote it to studying. She relied on court eunuchs to spy on her son and his wife, but her order wasn't always followed. Because of this, she separated the couple, isolating her son in the Qianqing Palace, one of the three halls of the inner court of the Forbidden City. Isolated, the young emperor was lonely and depressed, which led to him developing an ill-temper toward his servants, who he would often beat. When he could no longer stand the isolation, he started sneaking out of the palace and enjoying the pleasures offered by the unrestricted parts of Beijing. He would disguise himself as a commoner and spend his nights in brothels.

The Tongzhi Emperor proved to be an incompetent ruler. He hated studying, and by the time he became an independent ruler, he could barely read a full sentence from the official state documents. Because of his slow abilities to learn, he was given personal rule four years behind the usual age of sixteen, which started in November of 1873. During his rule, he made two major decisions of stately importance. The first one was to rebuild the Summer Palace that was destroyed during the Opium Wars. He wanted to gift them to Empress Dowagers Cixi and Ci'an, but historians agree that it was just an excuse to get rid of their influence in the imperial court. This project drained too much money from the royal treasury, so he ordered the nobles to invest with their own funds. As the construction of the palaces started, he began spending more and more time outside of the Forbidden City, indulging himself with various pleasures.

The second decision the Tongzhi Emperor made was to strip the Princes Dun, Chun, Fu, and Qing, as well as Grand Council members Li Hongzao and Shen Guifen, of all their offices and titles. Both Cixi and Ci'an tried to persuade him to change his mind, but their attempts proved to be futile. However, soon after, the emperor became ill. Rumor has it that it was syphilis, which he contracted during his brothel excursions. The official statement stated that he was suffering from smallpox. He died due to illness on January 13th, 1875, with Lady Arute, who gained the title Empress Xiaozheyi after her death, following in March.

The Tongzhi Emperor had no sons to inherit the throne. Since his uncles were all from a generation above his, they were considered to be unfit to rule according to tradition. This is why the first surviving son of Prince Chun became the new emperor. Coincidentally, he was also the son of Cixi's younger sister, Yehenara Wanzhen. The Guangxu Emperor was only four years old when he ascended to the throne in 1875. The child emperor was taken away from his home and was never again reunited with his family.

Not long after, Empress Dowager Ci'an suddenly died in 1881. Many believe that it was Empress Dowager Cixi who poisoned her because of their disputes. But that is just a rumor. Most historians accept the report of traditional Chinese medicine, which states that she died of a sudden stroke. Without the help of her friend and co-ruler, Empress Dowager Cixi resorted to written communication with the ministers. She even retreated from holding royal audiences, thus leaving the young emperor alone.

Cixi blamed Prince Gong for the loss in the Sino-French War, which lasted from 1884 to 1885 and was an undeclared war fought over the control of territories in Vietnam. Once again, she used her power to demote him to the position of advisor. She instead elevated Prince Chun to the higher positions since he was more easily manipulated.

According to Chinese imperial tradition, Emperor Guangxu obtained the right of personal rule at the age of sixteen. Cixi started preparing for the crowning ceremony, but intimidated by her prestige and power, court officials asked her to postpone the ceremony under the excuse that the emperor was still too young. Cixi accepted their suggestions and issued an edict that granted her the power to be the emperor's "aid" indefinitely. However, Cixi's prolonged regency did not stop the Guangxu Emperor from slowly starting to resume his duties. In 1886, he started adding his own comments to the imperial documents. By 1887, he started ruling under the supervision of Empress Dowager Cixi. When he got married in 1889, he finally became the sole ruler. For the emperor's wife, Cixi chose her own niece, Jingfen. She was also a cousin to the Guangxu Emperor, and she would later become known as Empress Longyu.

When the emperor went through the ceremonies that gave him reigns of imperial power, Cixi finally retired but still served as the head of the family. She retreated to the newly built Summer Palace to live out her retirement, but the emperor visited her every two to three days with other court officials. She was always sought to give advice for the most complex questions of politics, and this allowed her to keep having a great influence on state affairs.

When the previously described Hundred Days' Reform failed in 1898, Empress Dowager Cixi actually planned to remove the Guangxu Emperor from the throne, as she blamed him for plotting to kill her. She wanted to name Pujun, a close relative who was fourteen as the new crown prince. In order to avoid a scandal, Cixi was satisfied with removing the emperor from power but letting him keep his title. He was also placed under house arrest after losing all respect, privileges, and power. However, the Guangxi Emperor did play the role of emperor effectively. He was allowed to keep himself informed of all stately affairs but only in the presence of Empress Dowager Cixi. During audiences, he had to be present, and he sat on a little stool to the left of Cixi, who occupied the main throne. He had no real power to decide anything related to politics and wasn't even asked for advice. His tutors and supporters were either exiled or executed, leaving him without any company.

During the Boxer Rebellion, Empress Dowager Cixi, the Guangxu Emperor, and the rest of the court were forced to flee Beijing., returning again in 1902. At the time, Cixi started implementing political reforms throughout the empire. She sent officials to Europe and Japan to gather information about law, governmental structure, social policy, and education, among other issues. Finally realizing that China could not survive as a world political power while clinging to its traditions, Cixi initiated radical reforms. The most important reform was the abolishment of the imperial exams in 1905. Her hostility toward foreigners wasn't as strong at this point, and she started inviting the wives of foreign officials for tea in the Forbidden City. She hired a Western-educated lady-in-waiting to act as a translator on these meetings. Soon after, Cixi organized parties for the foreign community of Beijing at her Summer Palace, where she allowed a photographer to take photos of her and her court. Even though they were heavily staged photos designed to impress the world with Chinese imperial authority, aesthetics, and refinement, these photos are a unique window into the life of Empress Dowager Cixi, who ruled, with all the power of the state, for 45 years.

Photo of Empress Dowager Cixi (center) and the women of the American delegation

https://en.wikipedia.org/wiki/Empress_Dowager_Cixi#/media/File:The_Qing_Dynasty_Cixi_Imperial_Dowager_Empress_of_China_On_Throne_7.PNG

Empress Dowager Cixi died on November 15th, 1908, just one day after the Guangxu Emperor. Probably foreseeing her own death, she managed to install Puyi as the next emperor the day before she died. Forensic tests found an enormous amount of arsenic in the body of the Guangxu Emperor, and historians speculate that Cixi poisoned him to prevent his rise to power once she died because she knew her death was imminent.

She was buried close to her co-empress and longtime friend Empress Dowager Ci'an. Her tomb is a large complex of temples and pavilions covered in gold leaf. In 1928, warlord Sun Dianying and his forces plundered her tomb and threw her body on the floor. However, in 1949, the complex of the tomb of Empress Dowager Cixi was restored by the Chinese government.

Chapter 10 – Boxer Rebellion

Between 1899 and 1901, another uprising took place in China. The main goal of the rebels this time was to fight off foreign influence, including Christian missionaries. The rebellion was initiated by the Militia United in Righteousness, another Millenarian secret society. The members of this society were often skilled in martial arts; therefore, the foreigners, in particular, the Americans and British, named them the Boxers. This secret society practiced a type of spiritual possession, which they claimed made them immune to bullets, knives, and cannonballs. The movement was especially appealing to unemployed, impoverished villagers and teenagers.

However, anti-foreign sentiment wasn't their only reason for starting the rebellion. A series of drought and floods hit the northern provinces of China, causing famine and poverty to rise in areas that were inhabited by the Boxers. In addition, anti-imperial sentiment was on the rise, as the Qing dynasty wasn't able to provide assistance.

After the Opium Wars and the Self-strengthening Movement, China was divided into territorial spheres of influence by the Germans, Russians, British, and French. The foreigners had exclusive control over various industries, such as the mining and railway sectors. Germany held the Shandong province, while Russia had great influence over the provinces north of the Great Wall. France controlled the industries of the Yunnan, Guangxi, and Guangdong provinces, while Japan controlled Fujian. The British Empire had power over the Yangtze River Valley and the parts of Guangdong and Guangxi that weren't under France's influence or a part of Tibet. Many of the foreign governments opened up their own schools and churches and settled their own citizens in these provinces. The Russians even set up their own administration in several cities without the consent of the Chinese government.

The Treaty of Tianjin from 1858, which ended the Second Opium War, allowed foreigners to send missionaries, who would preach Christianity all over China. They were also allowed to buy properties and lands and open their own churches. On November 1st, 1897, one such church was attacked by members of the Big Swords Society, whose members were mostly peasants. Two German priests were killed in the attack, which is known as the Juye Incident. In October of the same year, another group of Boxers attacked a Christian community, which had converted the temple of the Jade Emperor into a Catholic church. During this incident, the Boxers used the slogan "Support the Qing, destroy the foreigners," a phrase they would later become known for. The main fear the Chinese had, after Germany took over the Shandong province, was that the European powers were trying to divide and colonize their country.

The start of the Boxer movement coincided with the Hundred Days' Reform of the Guangxu Emperor. The failure of these reforms only confirmed the ruling opinion that the foreigners were to blame for the national crisis that China was experiencing. After losing several wars to the foreigners, China was forced to accept unequal treaties that gave missionaries the freedom to spread Christianity, and the fact that foreign companies also gained special privileges and were exempted from Chinese laws could only cause resentment among the Chinese population. In 1900, it even appeared that China would be dismantled by Japan, Russia, Germany, and France. The Qing dynasty started losing its power while Chinese culture was being bombarded by foreign religions and foreign social norms.

Empress Dowager Cixi suddenly changed her view of the Boxers during 1900 and gave them her support. This caused protests from the foreigners inhabiting China. Encouraged by this royal support, the Boxers started spreading toward Beijing. On their way, they burned Christian churches, killed members of Christian communities, and intimidated any Chinese official who tried to oppose them. Frightened foreign diplomats in Beijing called for help from the foreign armies, and the Chinese government allowed 435 navy troops from other countries to enter Beijing in order to avoid an international political scandal. In June of 1900, the Boxers took control over the railway line that connected Beijing with Tianjin, meaning that Beijing was now isolated. However, it was still guarded well.

On June 11th, 1900, the Germans caught a young Boxer in their quarter of the city and immediately executed him. In response, the Boxers, numbering in the thousands, entered the city and started burning churches, cathedrals, and Christians as well. American Marines managed to defend the Methodist Mission, who took in refugees. The British soldiers ruthlessly killed several members of the Boxers, but their actions just increased the hostility of the Chinese population toward foreigners. As a result, the Muslim Gansu army and the Chinese commoners joined the Boxers in their rebellion and started killing the Chinese who had converted to Christianity.

The day before this incident happened, a second contingent of foreign troops was dispatched to Beijing. It counted 2,000 soldiers, and it was under the command of British Vice-Admiral Edward Seymour. They had the support of the Chinese minister of foreign affairs, an office that at the time was occupied by Prince Gong, a pro-foreign and pro-reform official. But the presence of this army angered Empress Dowager Cixi, who replaced Prince Gong with his brother, Prince Duan, who gave the Boxers his full support. He even became one of the strongest Boxer leaders, ordering the Qing army to attack Edward Seymour's troops. However, the army had received conflicting orders, and Seymour's troops gained passage from Tianjin to Beijing.

The joint forces of the Chinese irregular and imperial armies soon attacked the foreign troops from all sides. On June 18th, the Battle of Langfang was won by the Boxers but at great cost. Edward Seymour tried to retreat with his troops but was constantly under fire from Chinese artillery. So, Seymour decided to change the direction in which to approach Beijing and turned his army along the Beihe River, toward the Tongzhou district, but he was forced to retreat the very next day since the rebel forces were in even greater numbers there. They were running low on rations, ammunition, and medical supplies and were carrying over 200 wounded soldiers with them.

However, they were fortunate because, during their retreat, they happened upon the Great Xigu Arsenal, which was barely defended and had plenty of ammunition, food, and medical supplies. The desperate soldiers managed to seize the arsenal and decided to wait for rescue. On June 25th, help finally arrived. A regiment composed of Russian and British troops came to their rescue. Seymour and his troops were freed, and together with their rescuers, they returned to Tianjin.

Since they were cut off from Beijing, the Allied forces of the European countries had to reinforce themselves in Tianjin. They also captured the Dagu forts, which allowed them to control the paths to the city. Among the foreigners based in Tianjin was an American engineer who would later become the 31st president of the United States, Herbert Hoover. The Allied army of the Eight-Nation Alliance, which numbered over 55,000, started their march toward Beijing. This alliance consisted of the US, Great Britain, Germany, France, Austro-Hungary, Italy, Russia, and Japan. They sent an ultimatum to Empress Dowager Cixi, asking for China to give up all of their military power and financial affairs to them. However, she was defiant and called for battle, as she would rather face her ancestors knowing that she defended China. She ordered Beijing to prepare for a siege, but after receiving word about the fall of the Dagu forts, she ordered all foreigners, diplomats as well as civilians, to leave Beijing under military escort. Fearing that the Chinese army would just kill them, the foreign diplomats, as well as the civilians, declined to obey the Empresses' order.

On June 21st, 1900, Empress Dowager Cixi declared war against all foreigners. However, the governors who had command over the modernized Chinese armies, such as Li Hongzhang in Canton, Yuan Shikai in Shandong, and Liu Kunyi in Nanjing, refused to acknowledge the declaration of war. Some of them chose to remain neutral, but others helped the foreigners fight off the Boxers. Those who decided to stay neutral managed to keep southern China out of the conflict and were named the Mutual Protection of Southeast China.

The Beijing Legation Quarter was under siege for almost two months. The Chinese and Boxer armies dug up tunnels under the foreign compound and placed a number of mines inside them. The foreigners suffered heavy casualties due to these mines, as well as because of the lack of food and medicine. The Chinese soldiers set fires around the British Legation in order to frighten its inhabitants, but the Hanlin Academy, which contained invaluable books, caught fire and burned. This incident angered both sides, who kept blaming each other for the loss of such great treasures. When the Chinese armies failed to burn the British Legation, they built barricades around the whole Legation Quarter and started advancing, making the foreign defenders retreat gradually. The Chinese armies never tried a full-frontal attack, even though historians today claim they would have been able to kill every foreigner in the Legation Quarter within just one hour if they had done so. It was probably the fear of retaliation that stopped Empress Dowager Cixi from giving such an order.

On July 3rd, 1900, a combined force of British, American, and Russian soldiers launched an attack on the Chinese barricade around the Tartar Wall, the most crucial point of defense in the foreign quarter of Beijing. The Chinese were sleeping, as it was 3 a.m. when the attack took place, and were caught off guard. The foreign soldiers managed to kill twenty Chinese and expel the rest of them from the barricades. On July 17th, a truce was called after the Chinese government learned about the Allied force of 20,000 soldiers, which had just landed in China.

It was the Manchu general Ronglu who decided that it was impossible to fight the war on multiple fronts. He halted the transfer of artillery that was supposed to strengthen the siege of Beijing, and with this act, he saved the foreign legations and forced the imperial court to accept a diplomatic consensus. Ronglu and General Nie Shicheng continued to protect the foreigners and fight against the Boxers and Muslim Gansu Braves. They issued food and other supplies to the foreign compounds of Beijing, saving them from starvation. Ronglu and Shicheng kept the path for the Allied army clear, and this allowed them to quickly arrive in Beijing. But Ronglu tricked Nie Shicheng, as he hid the real orders from the palace that stated they should fight off the foreigners. Shicheng thought he was supposed to fight the Boxers, and soon, he was surrounded by the Allied forces, which then attacked him. Upon learning his mistake, he chose to end his life by walking into the range of Allied artillery at the Battle of Tianjin. The truce between the imperial court and the Legation Quarter lasted until August 13th when the Allied forces led by British Major General Alfred Gaselee finally arrived at Beijing.

The Beijing metropolitan area was defended by three divisions of Manchu bannermen, but two of them were under the command of anti-Boxer General Ronglu. The last one was under the command of Prince Duan, who was against the influence of foreign forces, and so, he joined the Muslim Gansu Brave and Boxer forces. Half of the forces under Prince Duan had no Western military training, even though they were given Western weapons. The Gansu Braves were also undisciplined and wore traditional Chinese uniforms, which offered no protection against modern weapons. The Chinese were decimated in the battle against the Allied forces of Japan (20,840 men), Russia (13,150), British Empire (12,020), France (3,520), USA (3,420), Germany (900), Italy (80), and Austro-Hungary (75). The British were the first to reach the Legation Quarter, but the image of the American soldiers climbing the walls of Beijing is perhaps the most iconic image of the Boxer Rebellion. The British Army relieved the foreigners who were under siege by the Chinese on August 14th.

Dressed as farmers in padded blue cotton garments, Empress Dowager Cixi, the Guangxu Emperor, and their small retinue fled Beijing in three wooden ox carts soon after the battle. Empress Dowager Cixi never admitted that they were retreating from the city; instead, they called it a "tour of inspection." They traveled for several weeks until they finally arrived at the capital of the Shaanxi province, Xi'an. They were deep in Chinese Muslim territory, which was defended only by the Gansu Braves. Since it was beyond the mountain passes, though, the foreigners could not reach them, and the Allied forces had no order to pursue the royal family.

For over a year, Beijing, Tianjin, and other important cities of northern China were occupied by an international expeditionary force. The French troops were busy ravaging the countryside around Beijing, and the Americans and British leading the Eight-Nation Alliance continued fighting the Boxers. Soldiers, civilians, and missionaries of all nations indulged themselves in the looting of Beijing, but the German, Japanese, and Russian troops were the most criticized for their cruelty.

After the fall of Beijing, many state officials pushed for the continuation of the war, claiming that China was still strong and could repel foreigners if it remained united. However, when the empress was offered to continue her rule and was assured that no territories of China would remain occupied, Empress Dowager Cixi agreed to peace. On September 7th, 1901, the Boxer Protocol was signed, ensuring peace between the Qing dynasty of China and the Eight-Nation Alliance. China was fined war reparations of 450 million silver taels (a Chinese unit of measurement) and also had to execute all the leaders of the Boxer Rebellion. The reparation was to be paid by 1940 with an interest of four percent. By 1939, China managed to pay over 668 million taels of silver, which is the equivalent of approximately one billion US dollars. Some of the money given to the US as part of the war indemnity was invested in the Boxer Indemnity Scholarship Program, which paid for the education of Chinese students in the US. Britain also had a similar program.

The Western powers finally realized that the only way to colonize China was through the ruling Qing dynasty, as they had an iron grip over the population. Empress Dowager Cixi finally initiated the much-needed reforms in order to modernize China, despite her earlier resistance. After the death of Empress Dowager Cixi and the Guangxu Emperor, Prince Regent Zaifeng, also known as Prince Chun, continued the reforms.

Chapter 11 – The Last Emperor

Photo of Puyi (or Pu Yi), the Xuantong Emperor, last emperor of China

https://en.wikipedia.org/wiki/Puyi

After the death of the Guangxu Emperor, a two-year-old boy named Puyi, who was chosen by Empress Dowager Cixi, became the new ruler. He was the son of Prince Chun, who was the brother to the late Emperor Guangxu. His parents did not know that their son was going to be the emperor until the procession of eunuchs and guards came to take him away from his home. Puyi screamed and cried as he was taken away from his parents, and to calm him down, his wet nurse was allowed to accompany him to the palace. He was able to see his father at least, as Prince Chun was named prince regent and was the one who carried the two-year-old Puyi to his coronation ceremony where he was named the Xuantong Emperor. Frightened by ceremonial drums and plays, Puyi cried. For the next seven years, the new emperor was forbidden from seeing his mother, Princess Consort Chun. The only mother figure he knew was his wet nurse, and he developed a special bond with her that would last until her death.

Puyi really had no time to be a child. His life changed overnight, and he was treated like an emperor from the beginning of his reign. Nobody dared to discipline him or develop a deeper emotional relationship with him. Over time, Puyi realized no one would say no to him and that all his wishes could be fulfilled. He grew up to be a sadistic person who liked to whip and punish his eunuchs and servants. Eventually, Puyi developed two personalities, one that expected everyone to bow down to him and loved to flog eunuchs and another that experienced closeness to someone, like when he was a baby and his wet nurse was allowed to breastfeed and cradle him. His wet nurse was named Wang Wen-Chao, and she was the only person who could calm him down or persuade him against his daily cruelties toward court eunuchs. But she only stayed with him until he turned eight, after which she was expelled from the court by Empress Dowager Longyu. Later, Puyi himself wrote how he had many "mothers" but never felt motherly love. Five imperial concubines belonging to the former emperor, with Empress Dowager Longyu as their chief concubine, acted as Puyi's mothers. He had to make a weekly visit to see them and report on his educational progress. Other than that, the former concubines showed no interest in Puyi and actually kept his real mother from seeing him.

The young emperor also never had any privacy. He was constantly surrounded by eunuchs, who would clothe him, wash him, open the doors for him, carry his sweets, and even blow into his food to cool it. Eunuchs were not humans to him but more like furniture. He thought that he could do anything he'd like with them and often made them eat dirt while he had his meals. However, the eunuchs profited from serving the emperor. The eunuchs would sell or eat all the food he did not eat himself. The emperor also received new garments every day, and the eunuchs would sell the old ones, which were made from the finest silk. There were a lot of treasures in the Forbidden City that the eunuchs would steal and sell on the black markets. Eunuchs were all around the palace, as they did a lot of the work. They were cooks, gardeners, cleaning personnel, and entertainers. They also handled the bureaucratic work of the government and served as imperial advisors and the emperor's earliest teachers. Eunuchs spoke in a very high-pitched tone and were forced to carry their severed parts in a small jar full of brine around their necks as proof that they were really eunuchs.

When he was a child, Puyi was allowed to learn only about the Chinese Confucian classics and nothing else. He did not have classes in science, mathematics, or even geography. As he would state later in his own biography, for a long time he could not even tell where Beijing was located. Finally, when he was thirteen, he was allowed to have a visit from his family. For the first time after many years, he saw his mother, but like any other subject, she had to stay a respectful distance away and even bow to him. He was also visited by his younger brother Pujie, who never even knew he had an older brother. When he was told he was going to visit the emperor, Pujie imagined an old gray man sitting on the throne. He was surprised to see a young boy and to learn this was his brother. Pujie stayed in the palace from that moment on as a playmate for the young emperor.

In 1911, the Xinhai Revolution started. Also called the Chinese Revolution, the uprising of the people from all spheres of society managed to overthrow the Qing dynasty and establish the Republic of China. The emperor was only six years old when he had to abdicate. The mutiny of the army garrison stationed in Wuhan was the incident that sparked the revolt, which quickly spread across the whole country, as people began demanding the end of the Qing dynasty that had ruled them for 267 years. General Yuan Shikai was ordered to crush the revolution, but the army wouldn't fight since the majority of citizens were against the Qing dynasty. Instead of fighting the revolutionaries, Yuan started negotiating with them. He promised he would arrange the abdication of the child emperor, but in return, he demanded to be elected as the first president of the Republic of China. He presented the terms of abdication to Empress Dowager Longyu, who took over the regency from Puyi's father, and she issued the edict of abdication on February 12th, 1912, officially ending Qing dynasty rule.

The "Articles of Favourable Treatment of the Great Qing Emperor after His Abdication" that Empress Dowager Longyu signed with the newly established Republic of China ensured that Puyi kept his imperial titles and was treated by the republic like a foreign monarch would. He was also allowed to stay in the northern part of the Forbidden City as well as and Summer Palace. He was allowed to keep all the eunuchs and other staff of the court, but no new servants were to be employed. The republic also promised to pay him four million silver taels annually, a sum that was never paid in full. This "salary" for the emperor was abolished completely after a few years. What's interesting is that nobody told Puyi he was not the emperor anymore, so therefore, he continued to act as one. Only after the death of Empress Dowager Longyu in 1912 did he become aware of the changes in the Forbidden City.

Yuan Shikai strived to start a new imperial dynasty. He even restored the empire briefly and proclaimed himself as emperor in 1915. He called himself the Hongxian Emperor and formally ruled China until March 22nd, 1916. He had been facing uprisings all over the country, as civilians, as well as the army, were firmly against imperialism. After only 83 days of ruling, Yuan Shikai abandoned the monarchy, but the angered population now called for his resignation as president as well. Yuan soon died of illness in June 1916.

When Puyi was thirteen years old, Sir Reginald Johnston, a Scottish diplomat, started serving as the emperor's tutor in the Forbidden City. He was hired by the president of the Republic of China, Xu Shichang, who believed that the monarchy would be restored one day. Young Puyi had never seen a foreigner before, and Johnston's features, namely his mustache, were very amusing to him. Under this new tutorship, Puyi finally started learning political science, history, and the English language. He started reading English books, such as *Alice in Wonderland* and philosophy texts. Johnston often told the young Puyi of his homeland, Scotland, which amazed the emperor to such an extent that he wanted to go and visit it. Puyi admitted he was intimidated by his new foreign tutor and felt respect for him that he could never feel for his Chinese teachers. This awe for Johnston made him willing to study more.

Johnston soon discovered that he could control the young emperor and often influenced him or persuaded him to abandon his capricious ideas. Even the eunuchs began to rely on him to deal with Puyi's behavior. Under the influence of his foreign tutor, Puyi chose a British name "Henry" (after the king of England) for himself and started speaking "Chinglish," a mixture of English and Mandarin. He also discovered the wonders of the cinema and ordered a projector for the palace. The eunuchs were very much against foreign technology but could not argue with the wishes of their emperor. Furthermore, Puyi was shortsighted, but he was never allowed to wear glasses as it was regarded as not being dignified for an emperor. Johnston argued this decision with Prince Chun and finally won. The emperor's foreign tutor was also the one who introduced Puyi to modern publications of China. He hired the writer Hu Shih to teach Puyi about the new developments in Chinese literature. Puyi wrote a few poems that were printed in the "New China" publications under a pseudonym.

Johnston influenced the way of life in the palace more than his title of tutor would suggest or allow. He introduced the bicycle as a healthier way for young Puyi to move about the Forbidden City, instead of being carried everywhere. Puyi loved cycling so much that it remained his lifetime passion. Under Johnston's instructions, Puyi reduced the waste of food and other extravagances in the palace, finally realizing that his servants needed to eat too. He learned how to open the doors for himself instead of expecting someone else to do it for him. Furthermore, the young emperor decided to cut off his Manchu queue and grow his hair in the Western style, and he also expressed a desire to study at Oxford. Johnston also introduced the first telephone into the palace, and Puyi loved it so much that he would often call random numbers just to hear the voices of other people on the other end.

In 1922, Puyi was married to Gobulo Wanrong, a daughter of a Manchu aristocrat. She wasn't his first choice for a wife, but under the pressure of the dowager consorts, he married her. He was informed that his first choice was only suitable to be his consort. Puyi tried to escape the Forbidden City on June 4th, 1922, an escape that had nothing to do with his future marriage: He just wanted to go to Oxford to study. He even planned to write an open letter to the people of China explaining his reasons and renouncing the title of emperor. Johnston was actually the one who stopped his flight. He simply refused to call for a taxi and go with Puyi, who was afraid of being alone on the streets of Beijing, let alone traveling to a foreign country. Even though Sir Reginald Johnston showed nothing but great affection for the young Puyi, he was of the firm belief that China needed an emperor and that the power of the imperial court would return with Puyi as the new ruler.

On October 21st, 1922, Puyi married Princess Wanrong, as well as to his consort, Wenxiu. The ceremony took place during the night, under the full moon, as Chinese tradition dictates that the moon brings luck to a marriage. After the wedding, Puyi, Wanrong, and Wenxiu went to the Palace of Earthly Tranquility, a place where emperors traditionally consummated their marriages. However, Puyi was young and inexperienced. Growing up surrounded by eunuchs, he had no knowledge of what was expected from him, and he fled, leaving the two women to spend the night alone. Puyi never fathered a child and had a series of unhappy marriages. This led people to believe he was homosexual. But there are no rumors of him having a male lover. Some believe he was just impotent. Since there are so many theories about his sexuality, it will probably always be shrouded in mystery.

In 1923, Puyi wanted to stop the corruption inside the Forbidden City. As his first measure, he ordered an inventory of the royal treasures. To cover up their stealing, the eunuchs set the Hall of Supreme Harmony on fire during the night of June 26th. The report of losses due to the fire included a significant number of statues, golden ornaments, porcelain antiques, and furs, but most of it was actually probably sold on the black market by thieving eunuchs. As a result of the fire and growing suspicions, Puyi expelled all the eunuchs from the palace, keeping only fifty of them to serve the dowager consorts, who claimed they needed them to live. The Forbidden City suddenly became empty, taking on an atmosphere of an abandoned and desolate place. In place of the burned palace, Puyi ordered a tennis court to be built for himself and his wife, Wanrong.

The coup of 1924, which saw the warlord Feng Yuxiang take control over Beijing, was an event that turned Puyi's life upside down. Feng decided to revise the "Articles of Favourable Treatment," and on November 5th, 1924, Puyi's titles and privileges were abolished. He was expelled from the Forbidden City and became a private citizen of the Republic of China. He sought refuge in a Japanese embassy in Beijing due to the advice of his tutor Johnston, who felt that the Japanese tradition of worshiping their emperor as a god would be a much more suitable environment for Puyi. However, the Japanese had plans of using and controlling Puyi. Eventually, they relocated him to the Japanese Concession of Tianjin, where they could easily monitor and influence him without the Chinese government meddling. On February 23rd, 1925, Puyi took the train for Tianjin, wearing a simple Chinese gown.

During his life in Tianjin, Puyi was often petitioned by various warlords and military generals, both Chinese and foreign, who promised to restore him to the throne if he would give them money. Puyi also loaned over 5,000 British pounds to Russian General Grigory Semyonov, but he never saw that money returned. Out of boredom, Puyi indulged in excessive shopping, which included the purchase of pianos, watches, shoes, and Western clothes. His first wife, Wanrong, started consuming opium due to their new lifestyle, and their marriage started falling apart. Wanrong was educated in the Western style, and she started resenting the life of an empress, which was filled with meaningless traditional protocols. She was young and loved dancing, jazz music, and Western fashion, and she started fully enjoying the life that the modern Republic of China had to offer. In 1928, Puyi's consort Wenxiu declared that she had had enough of him. She simply walked out of the Japanese palace in Tianjin and filed for divorce.

In 1931, Japan started the invasion of Manchuria after Puyi wrote to the Japanese minister of war expressing his wish to be restored to the throne. Japan offered to install him as emperor of the newly conquered Manchuria instead, and he accepted. Wanrong did not want to follow her husband, though, as she saw his actions as treasonous. It was Puyi's cousin, Eastern Jewel, who finally convinced Wanrong to follow her husband since it was her duty. Eastern Jewel, also known as Yoshiko Kawashima, was a Manchu princess who worked as a spy for the Japanese government. She was an interesting character as she was openly bisexual and often dressed as a man. Her spy career was over when she got too famous for her deeds and instead started appearing in newspapers and on the radio. As a celebrity, she couldn't possibly be any use as a spy, but she was used as a propaganda tool for pro-Japanese politics. She was arrested on November 11th, 1945, in Beijing. As she never renounced her Chinese citizenship, she was tried as a domestic traitor rather than a war criminal. In March of 1948, she was executed by a bullet in the back of her head after being convicted of treason.

Protected by the Japanese, Puyi left Tianjin for Manchuria, even though the Chinese government issued an arrest warrant for him, declaring him to be a traitor. When he arrived in Port Arthur, he met Masahiko Amakasu, a Japanese general known for his brutality on the battlefield. He bragged about killing women and children to Puyi, who slowly began to realize that he was a prisoner in Manchuria, as he was forbidden from leaving his hotel.

During 1932, the new state of Manchukuo was organized with Puyi as its chief executive. He was greatly disappointed that he wouldn't be referred to as "Your Imperial Majesty" and that he wouldn't be ruling with the Mandate of Heaven. He was calmed by Seishiro Itagaki, the Japanese war minister, who promised him that one day he would become emperor again. He also told him Manchukuo was just the beginning and that Japan had plans to conquer all of China and restore the Qing dynasty. Puyi believed that Manchukuo was just his temporary base, and just as his forefathers had done in 1644, he would lead an army and retake all of China. In Japanese propaganda, Puyi was represented as a Confucian king who would restore virtue. He was also presented as a revolutionary who would start modernizing the country. But Manchukuo was a puppet state of the Empire of Japan, and as such, the government had to do Japan's bidding.

In 1933, Puyi was told he was finally going to be installed as the emperor of Manchukuo. When he asked if he would receive the title of "Great Qing Emperor" back, he was disappointed to hear that the title only belonged to the emperor of Japan, Hirohito, who was now his father. Puyi was to obey the Japanese Kwantung Army since they represented the will of the Japanese emperor. Puyi was crowned on March 1st, 1934, in Changchun, his new capital city. Wanrong did not attend the ceremony, as her hatred toward Japan and her opium addiction could not guarantee her behavior to remain appropriate for the whole ceremony. Puyi was the only Chinese emperor who wore Western-style garments to his coronation ceremony. He could not agree with the Japanese officials, who wanted him to wear a

Manchukuo uniform instead of the traditional Manchu robes of the Qing dynasty. After the coronation, since Changchun had no palaces, Puyi, who was now addressed by the title Kangde, moved into the Salt Tax Palace, an administration building from when Russia was in Manchuria. There, he lived as a prisoner, heavily guarded by the Japanese army. He wasn't allowed to leave the palace without the permission of the Japanese generals.

As the head of state, Puyi had to sign documents and edicts. But he was told what to sign since the real decisive power came from Tokyo. With his signature on the documents, Puyi was directly responsible for the Japanese atrocities committed in Manchukuo. In addition, he signed documents in which Japan gained control over vast farmlands. The Kwantung Army also occupied entire districts in the capital city, while Puyi's Salt Palace was a small building next to the railroad and red-light district. Manchukuo was a true colonial state, and Japan was the only one profiting from it. Japan planned to populate Manchukuo with predominantly Japanese families and help control the overpopulation of their own country, so the Chinese and Korean farmers were evicted to make room for Japanese families, who arrived in great numbers. Anyone opposing the orders was used as target practice for the Kwantung Army. The Chinese workers were exploited in new factories and mines all over Manchukuo, and they were often dehumanized and treated as slaves.

Puyi's life as the puppet emperor of Manchukuo was filled with signing various documents prepared for him by Japan, consulting oracles, and reciting prayers. He also spent much of his time doing formal visits throughout the state, as well as being an active participant in various ceremonies. Gradually, he became aware that his "loyal subjects" hated him, and this knowledge, as well as the fact that he was a prisoner in the Salt Palace, drove him to the brinks of madness. His moods often changed, and he returned to his old practice of sadistically beating his servants.

Puyi's knowledge of what was happening outside his palace was scarce. He only knew what the Japanese officials would tell him, and he was unaware of the events of the Second Sino-Japanese War, such as the Rape of Nanking in December of 1937. The next year, 1938, Adolf Hitler recognized the state of Manchukuo, and the preparations for assembling a German embassy were underway. The newly renamed capital Hsinking (Changchun) only had the embassies of Japan, El Salvador, the Dominican Republic, Costa Rica, Italy, and nationalist Spain, all the states that recognized the sovereignty of Manchukuo.

In 1938, Puyi was declared a god, and schoolchildren began their classes with prayers to his portrait. The cult of emperor-worshiping was organized just like in Japan. It was decided that the citizens of Japan and Korea were devoted to their country and would sacrifice everything for their God-Emperor. In the light of the Second Sino-Japanese War, the same devotion was needed from the people of Manchukuo, as massive army recruitments were taking place. Becoming a god was hard for Puyi, as he was never allowed to leave his Salt Tax Palace. He was forced to sign a document in which any of his male children, if he ever had them, would be sent to Japan for their upbringing.

His wife Wanrong had developed an affair with Puyi's driver, Li Tiyu, by this point, and from that relationship, a girl was born. Japanese officials decided to poison the newborn baby, and to punish her, Wanrong had to watch her daughter die. Puyi was aware of what the Japanese planned to do to the child, but he couldn't do anything about it. Later, a ghostwriter who worked on his autobiography stated that Puyi couldn't talk about these events as he was too ashamed of himself. Wanrong lost all of her will to live after the death of her child and spent her days numbing her pain with opium.

Following the lead of Japan, Manchukuo declared war on the US and Great Britain in 1941. Puyi was an exemplary Japanese puppet during the war. On one of the rare occasions he was permitted to leave the palace, Puyi greeted the graduates of the Manchukuo Military Academy and awarded the best-performing cadet with a golden watch. This cadet was a Korean soldier named Park Chung-hee, who would later become the dictator of South Korea in 1961.

In 1942, Puyi lost his concubine, Tan Yuling, who he believed was poisoned by the Japanese doctors who killed Wanrong's daughter. For the rest of his life, he kept a lock of Tan's hair and her nail clippings as a remembrance, stating that she was very dear to him. Even though he was pressured by Japanese officials, Puyi did not want to take a Japanese concubine. Instead, he chose a lowborn sixteen-year-old Chinese girl named Li Yuqin.

For almost the entire duration of World War II, Puyi believed Japan was winning. He started doubting his beliefs only when Japanese propaganda started mentioning the heroic sacrifices of Burma and the Pacific islands. He gathered the courage to finally turn on a Chinese radio station and was shocked to learn how many defeats Japan had suffered. He secretly started hoping the Allies would win the war. In 1945, he was told that Russia had declared war on Japan and that the Red Army was entering Manchukuo. However, Japanese generals assured Puyi that they could easily defeat the Russians. When the Red Army, followed by the Mongolian army, entered the capital of Hsinking and overwhelmed the Kwantung Army, Puyi was hastily taken to southern Manchukuo by train. He observed the Manchukuo Imperial Army deserting in fear of the Red Army. The Japanese and Korean generals were actually among the first to leave the capital, if they hadn't already committed suicide. On August 14th, 1945, Puyi learned of Japan's surrender by listening to the speech of Hirohito over the radio. This was also his first time hearing about the bombing of Hiroshima and Nagasaki, as the Japanese generals never bothered to tell him. The very next day, Puyi abdicated as emperor, stating that Manchukuo was once again part of the Republic of China. He planned to escape by plane to Japan, leaving behind his wife Wanrong and his concubine. His brother's wife and their two daughters were also left behind. Puyi did not want to leave women and children behind, but the Japanese wouldn't take them as they saw the lives of men as more important. This was the last time Puyi saw Wanrong. However, instead of a Japanese plane coming to pick him up, a Russian one showed up. Puyi and his entourage were all arrested by the Red Army, and those he left behind were all captured by Chinese communists.

Wanrong was put on display in her jail cell, and people from all over the country came to see her. Under opium withdrawal symptoms, she started hallucinating, ordering her imaginary servants around and screaming for her dead daughter. Because she supported her husband, Wanrong was seen as a Japanese supporter and received no sympathy from Chinese officials or even the common people. They even stopped feeding her, and she died in 1946 of starvation, in a puddle of her own vomit and urine, with the people still coming to see her, laughing at the sight. Puyi learned of her death only in 1951, and he never mentioned whether he knew about the way she died.

The Russians took Puyi to a Siberian sanatorium in Chita and then to Khabarovsk, a spa center near the Chinese border, where he was treated well and was even allowed to have servants. Fearing that the Soviets would soon extradite him to China, Puyi wrote to Stalin, asking for asylum and for one of the palaces of the former Russian royal family. He never received any reply. However, the Russians refused to give him over to the Chinese, as he would've probably been executed. Puyi knew about the Chinese Civil War, which was fought between the government of the Republic of China and the Communist Party of China, since he was allowed to listen to the radio, but he never showed much interest in it. He spent his days in Russia praying to Buddha and being cruel to his servants and other prisoners.

In 1946, Puyi testified at the International Military Tribunal for the Far East, where the leaders of the Empire of Japan were put on trial for war crimes and conspiracy. Later, Puyi admitted he lied and hid the whole truth from this tribunal, as he was trying to save his own skin. When asked if he was kidnapped by the Japanese and taken to Manchukuo to be its emperor by force, Puyi replied that it was never his intention to leave China and that he did not leave Tianjin willingly.

After the negotiations between Russia and Maoist China, Puyi was transferred back to China in 1950. Mao Zedong, the leader of communist China, saw value in keeping Puyi alive. If he could break Puyi and remodel him to become a communist, no one could deny the power of the Chinese communist system. Even the Russians had to execute their royal family, meaning that even Lenin didn't wield as much power. This would make Chinese communism superior to any other on Earth. Puyi was afraid he would be executed in China since no one told him of the reeducation plan. Instead, he was brought to the Fushun War Criminals Management Centre, where he spent the next ten years until he was declared to be reformed.

In Fushun, prisoners bullied Puyi since he was not able to take care of himself. Even at the age of 44, he did not know how to tie his own shoelaces or brush his own teeth. He often left doors open and never made his bed, as he still expected others to do these trivial jobs for him. During his whole life, he never had to take care of himself; he always had servants who would bathe him, dress him, feed him, and so on. However, nothing serious ever happened to him because he was liked by the guards, particularly by the warden, Jin Yuan, who grew up in Manchukuo and bowed to Puyi's portrait when he was a child. He described Puyi as a very nice person and said he liked him very much.

In December of 1959, Puyi was allowed to leave the center as Mao regarded him as a successfully reformed man. Puyi was given a job as a street sweeper, and he had to live in an ordinary apartment building with his sister. On his first day as a sweeper, he got lost, as he had never walked the streets of Beijing before. After six months, he found employment at the Beijing Botanical Garden, where he said that he loved to work, as he found peace in gardening. He visited the Forbidden City together with other tourists who enjoyed hearing his stories of life at the palace. Puyi was often described by other people as an extremely nice person, to the point that he would miss a bus ride just because he would let everyone enter it before him. In cafes and restaurants, he would tell waiters that he should be serving them. Once, he accidentally hit an older lady with his bicycle, and while she was hospitalized, he would visit her and bring her flowers. He was also described as a very clumsy man who dropped things constantly. He had no idea how to use money and had to overcome the obstacles of everyday life with extra effort. In 1962, he married a nurse named Li Shuxian. He loved her very much and wouldn't leave her side when she was ill. He often told her that she was his whole world and that he would die if she left.

Puyi wrote his autobiography with the help of ghostwriter Li Wenda and was even encouraged by Mao Zedong himself. This autobiography had the purpose of promoting communism and tells the story of his endorsement of the new Chinese regime. The book was titled *Wode Qian Bansheng* (The First Half of My Life), but it was translated into English as *From Emperor to Citizen*. It took four years for Li Wenda to write the book based on Puyi's stories and interviews.

A few years later, Puyi died of kidney cancer and heart disease on October 17th, 1967, at the age of 61. His body was cremated according to Chinese laws. His ashes were placed next to other Communist Party dignitaries at the Babaoshan Revolutionary Cemetery. In 1995, Li Shuxian, Puyi's widow, transferred his ashes to the Hualong Imperial Cemetery, where they still lie next to the other emperors of the Qing dynasty.

Conclusion

After the Chinese revolution that brought down the last imperial dynasty, life for most Chinese citizens did not change. Some say that the only change they could observe was the currency, although the buying power of their wages stayed the same for the most part. However, the story is different for the Chinese elite, who saw the revolution as an event that would profoundly change their lives. Some loyalists to the Qing dynasty committed suicide, while others refused to cut off their Manchu queues. There was one aspect of the old culture that Qing supporters could not control, namely the ban on binding female feet, a practice that was considered aesthetically pleasing, even erotic.

The first attempts at creating a republic faced various difficulties. Many state officials were anxious over the loss of the central ruling figure and had a strong desire to return to the imperial system. For a long time, China struggled with implementing a new government that would push the multicultural country forward. Some ethnicities started desiring their own national identity and their own homeland. The Han Chinese acted as the only nation that had the right over China proper. These problems are still seeking a resolution today.

The collapse of the Qing dynasty in 1912 came at the right time when observed from a global view. The Russian Empire followed soon after in 1917 and the Ottoman Empire in 1922. The world was changing its political face, but were the people ready for that change? Puyi, China's last emperor, was the image of this much-needed change. He turned from the self-absolved child emperor, who enjoyed beating his eunuchs, to a completely reformed, kind, and gentle man. An emperor, who knew nothing but the riches of the palaces, became the man who lived humbly in a residential apartment in Beijing and cleaned the streets or took care of his garden. Puyi's life is a symbol of China's transition from empire to republic, and some of the wounds caused by it still haven't fully healed to this day.

Here are two other books by Captivating History that we think you would find interesting

References

Mao, H., Lovell, J., Lawson, J., Smith, C., & Lavelle, P. (2018). *The Qing Empire and the Opium War: The Collapse of the Heavenly Dynasty*. Cambridge, United Kingdom: Cambridge University Press.

Platt, S. R. (2018). *Imperial Twilight: The Opium War and the End of China's Last Golden Age*. London, UK: Atlantic Books.

Puyi, & Kramer, P. (2019). *The Last Manchu: The Autobiography of Henry Pu Yi, Last Emperor of China*. New York: Ishi Press.

Rowe, W. T. (2012). *China's Last Empire: The Great Qing*. Cambridge, MA: Belknap Press of Harvard University Press.

www.ingramcontent.com/pod-product-compliance
Lightning Source LLC
LaVergne TN
LVHW041644060526
838200LV00040B/1712